Isle

Colonsay

40 Coast and Country Walks

The authors and publisher have made every effort to ensure that the information in this publication is accurate, and accept no responsibility whatsoever for any loss, injury or inconvenience experienced by any person or persons whilst using this book.

published by
pocket mountains ltd
The Old Church, Moffat, DG10 9HB
pocketmountains.com

ISBN: 978-1-907025-58-7

A catalogue record for this book is available from the British Library

Printed in Poland

Introduction

The most southerly island group of the Hebrides, Islay, Jura and Colonsay have much to tempt the walker and traveller. Regular ferry services make this splendidly isolated group easy to reach, and the journey is rewarded by outstanding birdlife and wildlife, sandy beaches often bathed in sunshine, rugged hills, dramatic coastlines, fascinating historic treasures and – on Jura, but even more so on Islay – renowned whisky distilleries. You could easily spend a week on each of these islands and still leave many places unexplored, or a longer stay on Islay would allow enjoyable daytrips by boat to both Jura and Colonsay.

Featuring 40 walks, this volume aims to help you get the most from your visit to these islands. Most of the walks are a half day or shorter, with many suitable for families, but the guide also includes a few more challenging hillwalks for those who can't resist the allure of reaching an island summit. As you would expect, coastal walks dominate, with a rich variety – from wide sandy beaches such as Machir Bay on Islay or Kiloran Bay on Colonsay to stunning sea arches and the spectacular Soldier's Rock off Islay. Other routes explore the history of the islands, taking in sights such as the celebrated Kildalton Cross near Port Ellen or the sobering American Monument towering high above the seas on the Mull of Oa. The routes include the ascent to the highest points on all three islands – Islay's rough Beinn

Bheigier, the stony but awesome Beinn an Oir of the fabled Paps of Jura, and little known Carnan Eoin on Colonsay.

The routes are divided into five chapter areas, three of them on the larger Islay with a chapter each on Jura and Colonsay to complete the guide.

Safety

Although most of these walks are termed moderate, they often cross rough, pathless terrain and many of the routes can be wet underfoot. Choose sturdy footwear and carry waterproof clothing. The sketch map accompanying each walk is meant as an outline guide rather than a navigational aid, so for all but the most straightforward routes an Ordnance Survey map should be taken as well. The ascents of the Paps of Jura and Beinn Bheigier on Islay are proper mountain expeditions requiring hillwalking equipment and navigation skills.

Access

Scotland has fantastic access rights, some of the most progressive in Europe, thanks to the Land Reform (Scotland) Act 2003. This gives walkers the right of access over most land away from residential buildings and gardens. It is balanced with a set of responsibilities set out in the Scottish Outdoor Access Code.

On all three islands, sheep and cattle often graze on unfenced land or in fields along walking routes, and groundnesting birds are abundant. Therefore, dogs must be kept under strict control, especially in spring and early summer and whenever livestock is present. Even an encounter with a friendly dog can cause a ewe to abort a lamb and there have been cases of sheep being driven over cliffs by a free-running dog. Keep well away from cows with calves if you have a dog. The website outdooraccess-scotland.com has some useful advice on responsible behaviour, including wild camping. Deer stalking takes place on the hills (particularly on Jura) between 1 July and 20 October.

Ticks and midges can be a hazard during the summer months. The best precautions are to cover up by wearing long-sleeved tops and trousers, use insect repellent and check yourself thoroughly for ticks every evening, using a tick twister to remove any from yourself and any canine companions.

Transport

Caledonian MacBrayne (Calmac) operates regular ferries to Islay from Kennacraig on the Kintyre peninsula. The journey takes up to 2 hours 20 minutes to reach either Port Ellen or Port Askaig on Islay. A bus from Glasgow connects with the ferry at Kennacraig. Loganair operate direct flights from Glasgow and Hebridean Air Services run flights from Oban to Islay. Once on Islay, the bus operates a circular route along the main roads, taking in Port Ellen, the airport, Bowmore, Bridgend, Port Askaig, Port Charlotte and Portnahaven. Check the timetable as it changes during school

holidays, and no buses run on Sundays.

From Port Askaig on Islay it is just a 10-minute ferry ride to Jura. The council-run ferry runs hourly and Port Askaig is a 40-minute drive along the length of Islay from Port Ellen. There is a regular bus from the ferry to Craighouse and north to Inverlussa; check the timetable at the Garelochhead Coaches website. There are no buses on Sundays and the early bus only runs by request during school holidays and on Saturdays. There is also a summer passenger ferry from Tayvallich most days which takes under an hour and can carry bikes by arrangement.

Colonsay is served by a ferry three days a week from Oban; some of these ferries run on to Islay and Kennacraig and enable a daytrip to Colonsay from Islay once a week in the summer. Hebridean Air Services operate flights twice a week from Oban and Islay. Most people do not take a car to Colonsay as the island is fairly compact, and bike hire is available.

Wildlife

The mild winter climate has made Islay a popular destination for overwintering birds and this triggers a parallel migration of birdwatchers to the island. More than 37,000 barnacle geese and 13,000 white-fronted geese make Islay their winter home. These are easy to spot as they feed on Islay's rich farmland between October and April each year. With more than 200 species of bird on the island, the RSPB reserve at Loch Gruinart is an excellent place to start any birdwatching trip as there is an information centre, hides overlooking the water and wetlands where you can easily watch the wildfowl and perhaps spot a hen harrier or otter.

Islay is one of the few places on the British Isles where the rare chough breeds; Ardnave Point is a great place to see this red-legged corvid flying in small flocks. Breeding seabirds can be found on many of the higher cliffs on the islands, the Mull of Oa being a particularly dramatic spot. In summer months the elusive corncrake is on many birdwatchers' tick lists; their rasping call is heard much more easily than the bird is spotted – keep an ear and eye out around patches of nettles and flag iris on the edge of farmland. Colonsay and Jura are also good places to watch raptors and seabirds.

The coastlines of all three islands provide a rich habitat for seals and otters. Red deer are found on parts of Islay but, for guaranteed sightings, Jura is your island where the animals are said to outnumber the human population by 30 to 1.

History and culture

Islay and Colonsay are dotted with signs of very early human habitation, some dating back to 8000BC, including the remains of a roundhouse, numerous standing stones, early Celtic crosses, and also forts and other remains dating back to the Iron Age. At a time when the seas were the world's highways, Islay's position sitting far west between mainland Scotland and Ireland made it an important settlement.

When Norse invaders and traders arrived many stayed and the islands came under Norse control, ruled from the Isle of Man. This remained the case until the descendants of Somerled took control and used Finlaggan on Islay as their base. Here the MacDonald chiefs ruled as the Lords of the Isles from the 12th century for almost 400 years. From the early 1600s the Campbells ruled Islay and Jura, their dominance lasting well into the 20th century, a time of mass emigration fuelled by the Clearances, food and work shortages and the opportunities offered elsewhere. The First and Second World Wars also took their toll on the populations of the islands, though there has been a revival in the fortunes of all three islands in recent years.

One of the big draws for visitors to Islay and Jura today are the nine distilleries. Thought to have been introduced to the islands by Irish monks in the 14th century, Islay is particularly well suited to whisky production, with copious quantities of water, peat for fuel, and fertile land for growing barley. Today Islay's eight distilleries produce more than 20 million litres of whisky a year. Not to be outdone, Colonsay now has a thriving brewery producing real ales. In addition to the whisky industry, farming and crofting, supplemented with other work, and tourism are the mainstays of the local economy.

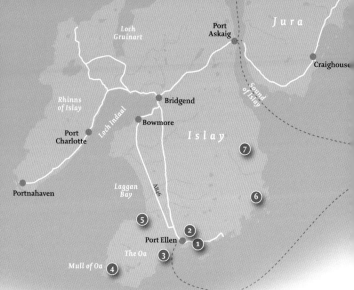

The whitewashed buildings of Port Ellen, curved around its sandy bay, are often the first sight for Islay visitors arriving on the Calmac ferry. If peaty whisky is your passion then the off-road walkway that runs from here to the three distilleries along the south coast (also known as the Kildalton Distilleries) – Laphroaig, Lagavulin and Ardbeg – will be an irresistible draw.

Shorter walks explore the farming countryside that still supplies grain for the malt, as well as uncovering evidence of Islay's prehistoric past with standing stones dating back to the Neolithic or early Bronze Age and the spectacular 8th-century Celtic carved cross at Kildalton.

A climb to the island's highest summit – Beinn Bheigier – should not be underestimated, as the challenging terrain makes this much more of an expedition than its 491m height would suggest.

The rugged southwest peninsula of Islay is known as the Oa. Once home to a scattered population of subsistence farmers, it is now largely uninhabited, its dramatic coastal cliffs home to many seabirds, including a colony of puffins, whilst the remote hinterland provides an ideal hunting ground for hen harriers and eagles. The Mull of Oa provides a poignant reminder of the power of the sea and the folly of man – the impressive clifftop American memorial commemorates the lives of more than 500 US seaman lost in two shipwrecks during the First World War. Other walks venture further along the coastline, visiting the Singing Sands and the Soldier's Rock, Islay's finest sea stack.

Port Ellen and the Oa: Southern Islay

The Kildalton Distilleries tour

Distance 6.25km **Time** 2 hours (one way)
Terrain tarmac path, short sections of
minor road with no pavement
Map OS Explorer 352 **Access** bus from
Bowmore to Port Ellen; bus from Ardbeg
to Port Ellen to return

Islay is world famous for its peated
whisky and this off-road pathway is the
ideal way to visit three iconic waterside
distilleries without having to worry
about having a sober driver amongst you.
The last distillery, Ardbeg, has a fine café
and there's a bus back if you don't fancy
making the return ramble. Check the
times and book in advance if you want to
tour any of the distilleries.

Most visitors arrive on Islay courtesy of
the ferry into Port Ellen. This small
settlement is Islay's second largest town
with a few facilities and a seafront main
street overlooking the white sandy beach

and safe anchorage of the bay. The former
distillery here now serves as a grain
maltings, providing malted barley for
many of the eight distilleries currently
operating on the island. The walk starts
along the grassy seafront with the bay on
your right; soon after passing the Co-op
supermarket, take the road (A846) on the
left signed for Ardbeg.

The road climbs and passes the school
on the edge of Port Ellen. Take the shared
cyclepath which runs parallel to the road
on the right-hand side, with good views
soon opening out to the sea. Shortly after
passing the Old Excise House on the left,
you can detour to the right to visit the
McDougall Monument.

Occupying a grassy mound overlooking
the sea, the cairn commemorates Islay-
born soldier and statesman Major General
Alexander McDougall. The McDougall
family emigrated when Alexander was six

and settled in Manhattan where he went to work as a milk delivery boy before signing up as a seaman. He worked his way up to become the owner of several merchant ships before being commissioned in the Continental Army during the American War of Independence. He later became a politician and president of the Bank of New York. MacDougal Street in Greenwich Village – famous hang-out of the Beat poets in the 1960s – is named after him.

Soon the first signs of distilling are seen as you approach the warehouses of the Laphroaig Distillery. After a short wooded section, turn right at the surfaced road to visit the distillery itself. Laphroaig is celebrated as one of the peatiest whiskies in the world, a real love-it-or-hate-it product worshipped by some whilst compared to drinking cough mixture by others. Whatever your taste, the distillery buildings are nestled in a beautiful shoreside setting and are worth exploring.

To continue the walk, return to the pathway and turn right, soon running parallel to the road and crossing open countryside for just over 1km before reaching Lagavulin Distillery. One of the oldest distilleries on Islay, it was registered in 1816, but distilling took place here illegally much earlier than that. It is thought that there were two distilleries founded here in 1816, the other taking the name of 'Kildalton'.

Continue along the road through the tiny settlement of Lagavulin until you can pick up the off-road route on the right-hand side. It climbs a small hill and crosses to the far side of the road before descending slightly to reach the grand entrance to Ardbeg Distillery. This is where the bus stops if you need to catch it for the return to Port Ellen. Like many of the distilleries on the island, Ardbeg was closed for many years, reopening in 1998. It now reaps the benefits of the renewed interest in single malts and has a cult following amongst whisky buffs. In addition to tours and a tasting bar, Ardbeg has a popular café and the buildings boast an enviable seafront location. If you've missed the bus, the return route is the same way.

◄ Ardbeg Distillery

The Standing Stones of Port Ellen

Distance 5km **Time** 2 hours
Terrain main road with no pavement for a
short distance, then quiet country lanes
Map OS Explorer 352 **Access** bus from
Bowmore to Port Ellen

**Explore the pleasant farming countryside
above Port Ellen on this circuit around
country lanes that takes in three ancient
standing stones. Facilities are available in
Port Ellen which also has a fine beach.**

Most visitors to Islay arrive via Port
Ellen's ferry terminal and are treated to a
lovely view of the colourful houses,
crescent-shaped sandy beach and distillery
building. It is the largest town on the
island after Bowmore, but still has the feel
of a small and quiet village, and is a
popular accommodation base for visitors.
If driving, there is parking in the village

centre, where the houses face the grassy
shore and beach. From here take the main
road past the Co-op supermarket on the
left and soon turn left along the A846
Ardbeg road, heading uphill and passing
the school.

As you keep following the road, watch
out for any drivers unfamiliar with the
protocol for single-track roads – they may
suddenly veer onto the wrong side of the
road in their urgency to reach a passing
place or avoid a wandering sheep. The first
turning to the left is the return route, so
stay on the main road until you are almost
at the prominent Old Excise House where
the warehouses of Laphroaig Distillery can
be seen directly ahead; take the road to the
left just before the house. As this road
climbs gently, it becomes apparent why
Islay developed such thriving whisky and
agricultural industries. The fertile fields are
lush green and perfect for growing the
grain needed for the distilling process. The
maltings that supply most of the
distilleries on the island are housed in the
buildings of the old Port Ellen Distillery.

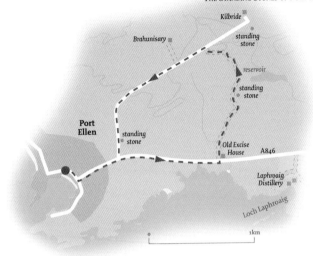

Kilbride

standing
stone

reservoir

standing
stone

Brahunisary

Port
Ellen

standing
stone

Old Excise
House A846

Laphroaig
Distillery

Loch Laphroaig

0   1km

Founded in 1825 as a malt mill, Port Ellen produced whisky for two periods in its life; the last drop was distilled in 1983 and is now very collectable due to its rarity.

After passing a house and continuing up the lane, look out for a stile on the right-hand side which provides access to the first standing stone. There are a number of standing stones dotted across Islay, which date from the Neolithic or early Bronze Age. Their purpose remains a mystery, although theories suggest they may have been route markers (these examples near Port Ellen seem a little large for this purpose), battle memorials or have some sort of calendrical significance, lining up with markers such as stars or sunrises and sunsets on specific dates.

The lane curves to the left before it reaches the tiny Port Ellen to Kilbride road; the route described turns left here. However, it is possible to turn right for a short detour to view another standing stone in the field opposite Kilbride farmhouse. Afterwards, turn around and follow the undulating road as it heads back towards Port Ellen.

A variety of grassland birds such as curlews, oystercatchers and lapwings can be seen and heard in the fields during the summer. On a clear day there are good views across the sea to Kintyre and you can often make out the jagged mountains of Arran beyond.

You soon come to the final standing stone on the left, just before the lane meets the main road. This one – a huge lump of local schist – stands a little over 4m high. At the main road turn right to retrace your steps to Port Ellen.

◀ Standing stone

Carraig Fhada and the Singing Sands

Distance 4.5km **Time** 2 hours
Terrain track, rough path, sand, optional
paddle to cross the burn on the beach
Map OS Explorer 352 **Access** no public
transport to the start

The unusual and distinctive lighthouse
of Carraig Fhada guards the entrance to
Kilnaughton Bay and Port Ellen. This fine
coastal exploration combines a visit to
the lighthouse with two sandy beaches,
including Traigh Bhan where your
scuffling feet may be able to make the
sands sing.

The walk starts across the bay from Port
Ellen. Take the Oa road past the distillery
buildings and immediately after the
cemetery turn left and, if driving, find a
parking place at the side of the track. From
here walk back along the road towards Port
Ellen for a short distance, turning right
before the woods to take a track which
emerges at the east end of Kilnaughton Bay.

As you arrive on this sandy beach, you'll
see the remains of a bathing hut over to
your left. The hut, now a ruin, would have
been used by the ladies of Cairnmore

House to change in before a bracing swim.
Aim to the right over the sands, crossing a
burn which may require a paddle (this can
be avoided by instead heading down the
surfaced lane from the parking area to join
the route at the south end of the beach).

Once at the far end of the sands, bear left
to follow the road along the shore. At a
bend, before the road starts to climb, keep
straight ahead, following the coastal track,
aiming for the lighthouse at Carraig Fhada.

These small white twin towers are a
prominent landmark when seen from the
Calmac ferry as it swings round to its berth
in Port Ellen. Viewed closer up it is possible
to appreciate the intricate detail of the two
connected square towers. A small bridge
and concrete path allows access to the base
of the first at all but the highest tide. Take
care in slippery conditions and keep an eye
out for the otters which also like to visit
these rocks. The lighthouse was
commissioned by Walter Frederick
Campbell as a memorial to his wife, Lady
Ellinor Campbell, in 1832, before being
taken over by the Northern Lighthouse
Board in 1924.

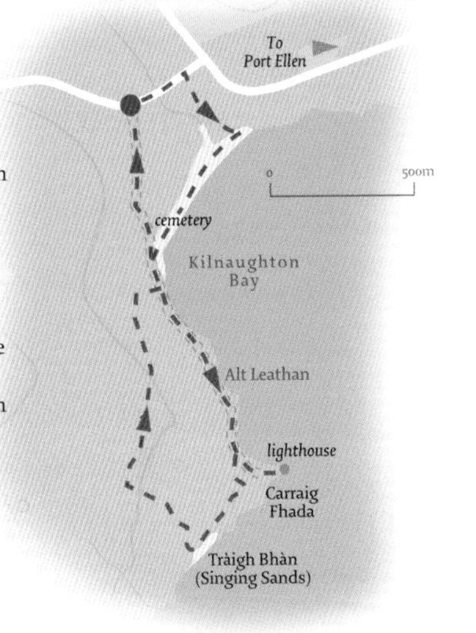

For the walk to the Singing Sands, return along the track until a green marker post indicates the start of the path just beyond the last building. Go through two sets of gates and follow the path along the coastline to reach the beautiful beach of Traigh Bhan. The 'singing' comes from the sound the sand makes as you walk through it, a phenomenon associated with the size of the grains of sand and also found on similar beaches on Ardnamurchan and the Isle of Eigg.

To return, you can retrace the outward route or, if you fancy a slightly tougher walk, take a faint path that heads inland from the back of Traigh Bhan on the far side of the burn flowing out onto the beach. The path climbs to reach a track; bear right along this with good views over the lighthouse to Port Ellen. Soon you meet a surfaced road where you turn left to return to the start – or turn right for a short detour to visit the remains of an ancient chapel in the first cemetery on the right. Be sure to seek out the knight, carved into a slab, clutching his sword.

To Port Ellen

0   500m

cemetery

Kilnaughton Bay

Alt Leathan

lighthouse

Carraig Fhada

Tràigh Bhàn (Singing Sands)

◄ Carraig Fhada Lighthouse

13

Mull of Oa and the American Monument

Distance 3.5km **Time** 1 hour 30
Terrain waymarked moorland and clifftop
paths, can be muddy in places
Map OS Explorer 352 **Access** no public
transport to the start

The high, rugged cliffs of the Oa are
made even more dramatic by the
American Monument, commemorating
the loss of more than 500 US servicemen
in two separate shipwrecks near the end
of the First World War. This waymarked
walk explores the high cliffs of the
RSPB reserve.

The Oa is the name given to the rocky
and rugged peninsula in the southwest of
Islay. Once fairly densely populated there
are now only a few scattered inhabited
houses and the headland itself is a nature
reserve. To reach the car park take the
signed road just west of Port Ellen,
passing the distillery buildings and
continuing to the very end of the public
road where there is an information board
and picnic tables.

Start by following the track west and,
at a bend, go through the kissing gate to
follow the path on the right. After a
second gate the path heads through open
pastures. Keep the fence on your left,
eventually taking the path which bears
right to reach a third kissing gate.
The lofty American Monument, standing
like a lighthouse on the high cliffs, can
now be seen ahead.

The monument commemorates those
lost in the sinking of two US troop ships

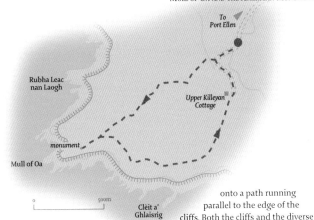

in 1918. The SS Tuscania, a requisitioned passenger ship carrying more than 2000 servicemen, was torpedoed by a German U-boat on 5 February, about 11km off the coast. More than 200 American and British crew were drowned when the ship sank several hours later, some during the perilous rescue operation. This was one of the biggest losses of life in the US military since the American Civil War, and the tragedy had a big impact in the USA.

Only eight months later, disaster struck again when HMS Otranto sank at Machir Bay, following a collision in bad weather with another troop ship. This time more than 431 people lost their lives, including 80 British crew. The memorial was erected two years later by the American Red Cross. Standing more than 10m high on the very edge of the cliffs, it can be seen from far out to sea.

From the monument retrace your steps for a very short distance and then turn onto a path running parallel to the edge of the cliffs. Both the cliffs and the diverse habitat inland support a wide array of birdlife. Look out for the rare choughs, crows with distinctive red beaks and legs. Hen harriers, golden eagles and peregrine falcons are also known to hunt in this area. From your vantage point above the sea you may be lucky enough to spot the hulking shape and double fin of a basking shark in the summer months.

Looking ahead, the distinctive headland of Dun Athad, once home to an Iron Age fort, can be seen projecting seawards whilst Beinn Mhor, the highest point on the Oa peninsula, is visible further off.

Go through a kissing gate and then aim diagonally to the left away from the cliffs to reach another kissing gate. The path leads towards the white farmhouse at Upper Killeyan with marker posts indicating the route. Another gate brings you onto a track which passes to the right of the house. Take the right-hand fork to return to the car park along the track.

◀ The American Monument at the Mull of Oa

The Soldier's Rock

Distance 8km **Time** 4 hours
Terrain track, coastal path, rough pathless
boggy sections, livestock grazing
Map OS Explorer 352 **Access** no public
transport to the start

One of the most spectacular stretches of
this coastline is the reward for a boggy
and pathless approach walk. Relatively
few visitors see the Soldier's Rock – Islay's
most impressive sea stack – enjoyed here
from the vantage point of a natural arch.

To reach Kintra take the Oa road from
Port Ellen, passing the distillery buildings
and then forking right for Kintra. Don't
park in the farmyard; instead there is a gate

on the right and, just beyond this, near the
entrance to the small campsite, is a parking
area. Start the walk by bearing left at the
track junction to head west; there are views
to the right across the vast 8km sweep of
sand at Laggan Bay. Soon the track swings
inland. Stay on the main track, shortly
crossing a burn, to eventually reach a
ruined house at Frachdale.

Turn right at the ruin on a muddy track
that starts to climb with great views over
Laggan Bay – note the standing stone to
the right. Pass through a gate and soon
you come to the end of the track at the
ruins of the village of Ghrasdail. Prior to
the 1830s there were many settlements like

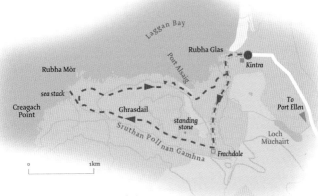

this across the Oa which had a population of more than 800. A combination of factors led to its depopulation – the new planned village at Port Ellen was built, providing a better standard of housing and local employment, some areas were cleared to make way for sheep grazing, and local food shortages combined with the industrialisation of Scottish cities lured others to move to Glasgow or try their luck in the New World.

The route now continues west through the ruins, aiming for the coast and very gradually descending to the waters of the Sruthan Poll nan Gamhna. Cross the burn before it runs into the deep ravine leading to the sea, and with care follow the path on the other side.

This crosses a large sea arch to reach a grassy headland with fabulous coastal scenery on both sides. Although the arch and ravine are impressive, it is the high sea stack known as the Soldier's Rock which draws the most attention. Like most sea

stacks this one would have begun life as part of the main island and has remained standing whilst weaker stone has been eroded by the action of the sea.

When you have soaked in the atmosphere of this wonderful spot, return over the arch to the burn crossing point and continue east along the coastline. There are a number of small paths through the heather and bracken; keep well above the coast to find the easiest route. When you come to a fence, drop downhill to a gate. The area after the gate is used for cattle grazing and is often muddy; pick your way through two copses of low trees and then aim for the left of a small concrete watertank, keeping well above the sandy beach at Port Alsaig. Bear northeast over grassy hummocks, picking up the remains of a track to eventually cross the burn near the outward route. A left turn here brings you back to the start.

Kildalton Cross to Port Mor

Distance **2.75km** Time **1 hour (round trip)**
Terrain **good farm track**
Map **OS Explorer 352** Access **no public
transport to the start**

**The impressive ancient carved cross in
Kildalton graveyard is the starting point
for this gentle walk to the shoreline
overlooking Ardmore Point. This is a
peaceful place to try and spot some of the
local wildlife.**

To reach the start take the A846 from
Port Ellen, passing the Ardbeg Distillery
and continuing along the minor road
beyond. The Kildalton Cross is looked
after by Historic Scotland and is signed
from the road. There is a parking area
adjacent to the ruined church; the cross
can be seen in the adjoining graveyard.

This early Christian cross is renowned
for the quality and detail of its 8th-
century carvings. It is believed the same
carver may have been responsible for
some or all of the three high crosses at
Iona. This Celtic, or ring, cross has
intricate carvings on both sides,
including depictions of Cain slaying Abel,
Abraham sacrificing Isaac, the Virgin and
Child, four lions and a snake, as well as a
peacock eating grapes – this final detail is
also found in the *Book of Kells* which was
produced at Iona Abbey. The cross stands
well over 2.5m high, its fine state of
preservation due to it having been carved
from local grey-green chlorite schist
which is extremely hard and durable.

Archaeologists believe that the cross is
still in its original position, withstanding

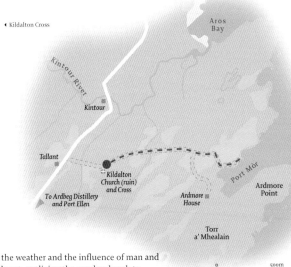

◀ Kildalton Cross

Aros Bay

Kintour River

Kintour

Tallant

Kildalton Church (ruin) and Cross

To Ardbeg Distillery and Port Ellen

Ardmore House

Port Mor

Ardmore Point

Torr a' Mhealain

0   500m

the weather and the influence of man and beast, outliving the nearby church to remain standing for more than 1200 years. By 1862 the cross was leaning at a perilous angle and work was undertaken to re-erect it. During the work a smaller cross and the bodies of a man and woman were found buried beneath the large cross. The ruined church is understood to have been used between 1200 and 1700.

Leaving the graveyard, walk down the track from the church and pass through the gateposts for Ardmore House; the 'Private' sign here refers to vehicles. The mixed woodland includes a number of old trees twisted and contorted by the wind and weather into natural sculptures.

When the main drive leading to the house bends right, stay on the track continuing straight ahead. Roe and fallow deer are often seen on this stretch; Islay has pure-bred red deer too, although Jura is the place to go to see large numbers of these bigger beasts.

The track meets the shore at Port Mor and reaches a private boathouse and jetty. This is an idyllic spot to sit and watch for seabirds and perhaps spot an elusive otter; however, please respect the privacy of the owners. The return route is back up the track to retrace your steps to the ruined church and cross.

Beinn Bheigier

Distance 16.5km **Time** 8 hours 30
Terrain lower slopes very wet with
difficult pathless walking, rocky ground
higher up **Map** OS Explorer 352
Access no public transport to the start

The highest point on the island makes a
great objective for a full day walk with rich
rewards in views and solitude. It is more
challenging than its relatively diminutive
height might suggest, however, due to the
very boggy and rough terrain underfoot.
High bracken in late summer can make
the walk even more difficult.

Take the road east from Port Ellen and
continue past Ardbeg Distillery and
Kintour to the end of the road at the north
end of Claggain Bay where there is a
parking area on the right. Start the walk by
heading through the gate and following
the track past the house at Ardtalla. Go
through a gate and stay on the track which
is usually wet underfoot. The track divides
into a number of options, but it doesn't
matter which one you take, they all climb
over Maol Ardtalla and cross equally boggy
ground before rejoining. Go through
another gate and descend to cross a bridge
over a burn. The path works its way above
the coastline, crossing a number of burns
before reaching the shore after Rubha
Biorach. The bothy at Proaig comes into
view and, as you approach, look for a
makeshift bridge to get you across the

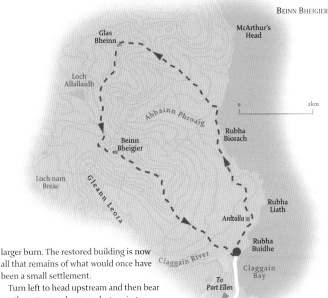

larger burn. The restored building is now all that remains of what would once have been a small settlement.

Turn left to head upstream and then bear northwest across hummocky terrain to reach the ridge between Gleann Coire Liunndrein and Gleann Dubh. This area is popular with red deer and you may spot herds roaming the hillsides. Careful navigation is needed throughout the climb, although the conditions underfoot become eventually drier and the ground stonier. After some time you curve west and then southwest to gain the summit of Glas Bheinn.

From here a bumpy ridge leads south, then southwest and south again to pass over Am Mam before descending to a wide bealach. For the final push to the summit of Beinn Bheigier aim to the right at first to avoid an area of scree before heading for the summit cairn. This is the highest point

on Islay; at 491m above sea level it provides excellent views on a clear day.

From the summit head southeast on the ridge to another cairn at spot height 456m. Bear south to descend the Diollaid nam Fiadh, ignoring the cairn on the east side. Once you leave the rocky ground behind, the route again becomes a tangle of grassy hummocks, bog and bracken. Keep to the right-hand side of a fence and, when another fence bars the route, turn right to reach a gate a short distance away. Soon you pick up a good track; follow this through a gate to the minor road at Claggain Bay and a short way to the left is the parking area at the start.

◀ Beinn Bheigier summit with view to Jura

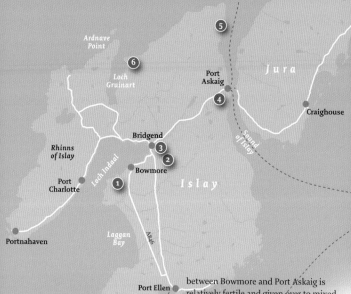

Bowmore is the largest town on Islay, providing all the major services for the 3000 residents, but it still retains the charm of a small village. Its rising High Street is dominated by the fascinating Round Church at its top end. The bottom end of the street reaches the sheltered harbour on Loch Indaal, once used by steamers from Glasgow to offload passengers. The shores of the shallow loch are popular with waders and seabirds and can be explored on a circular walk from the town.

The land stretching across the island between Bowmore and Port Askaig is relatively fertile and given over to mixed farming, whilst wilder moorlands lie to the north. Here is Finlaggan, the ancient seat of the Lords of the Isles for much of the 13th and 14th centuries; a visit on the way to Ballygrant or Bunnahabhain is repaid as much by its beautiful island setting as by its ruins, carved graveslabs and other finds displayed in the visitor centre. The wooded parkland which surrounds Islay House makes for an easy stroll, as do the fishing lochs set in the trees between Ballygrant and Port Askaig.

To the north of Port Askaig, the coastline is home to two of Islay's distilleries, Caol Ila and Bunnahabhain, with the latter being the start of a tough coastal hike to Rhuvaal Lighthouse at the northern tip of the island.

Bowmore's Round Church ▶

Bowmore and Port Askaig: Central Islay

Laggan Point

Distance 14km **Time** 4 hours
Terrain paths, tracks and 1.5km return
section on busy road with no pavement
Map OS Explorer 352 **Access** bus from
Portnahaven, Port Charlotte, Port Ellen
and Port Askaig to Bowmore

Explore the coastal promontory
southwest of Bowmore, with great
wildlife-watching opportunities.
The walk also visits a sandy beach before
returning inland. If you want to omit the
section of main road, you could instead
retrace your steps from Laggan Point
to the start.

Bowmore – the attractive capital of Islay
– is dominated by the intriguing Round
Church which stands at the top of the main
street. The village itself dates from 1768
and was originally planned to house
villagers uprooted when their homes were
deemed to stand in the way of the grand
parkland development planned for Islay
House near Bridgend. The Round Church is

well worth a visit – it is usually open
during the day, except during services.
Surprisingly large inside, it can seat up to
500 people, many of them in an upstairs
gallery. The initial congregation would
have consisted of the agricultural workers
and weavers who lived in the new planned
village. Within 10 years the distillery at
Bowmore had opened, bringing with it new
sources of employment and starting a
trend that would see eight more distilleries
open on Islay within the next century.

Start the walk from the Round Church,
taking the main road towards Port Ellen.
This climbs uphill for a short way, passing
the last few houses and then the bonded
warehouses where some of the distillery's
whisky matures in thousands of barrels –
though much more is aged in similar
warehouses on the Scottish mainland.

Beyond the warehouses turn right
down a minor road, heading towards the
coast. Turn left at the bottom of the hill
to follow a lengthy lane past the recycling

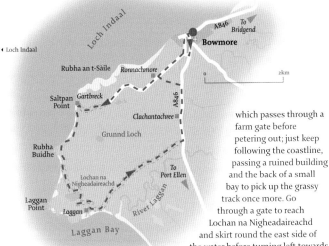

◄ Loch Indaal

which passes through a farm gate before petering out; just keep following the coastline, passing a ruined building and the back of a small bay to pick up the grassy track once more. Go through a gate to reach Lochan na Nigheadaireachd and skirt round the east side of the water before turning left towards some houses at a T-junction. Opposite a house, turn right along a stony track to pass Laggan Farm where there are soon wide views to the long sands of Laggan Bay ahead in the distance.

When the track starts to swing inland, you can detour to the right to visit a lovely sand and pebble beach which is a good spot for a break. Otherwise follow the track inland to eventually reach the main road. There is no pavement, so cross with care and turn left to face the oncoming traffic. After 1.5km look out for a track on the left; though a little overgrown in summer, it enables you to avoid the final stretch of road. The track joins the outward route near Ronnachmore; turn right here and, just before you reach the bonded warehouses, turn left for the centre of Bowmore.

centre and through farmland with good views over Loch Indaal to Port Charlotte. This stretch of relatively shallow water was home to a squadron of flying boats that patrolled the North Atlantic during the Second World War. The fierce winter storms presented an ongoing challenge to the air force and in January 1943 a fatal accident claimed the lives of nine airmen; soon afterwards the base was relocated to Northern Ireland.

After the recycling centre, the lane aims right towards the farm at Gartbreck. Just before the farm buildings, turn left in front of a fence to reach a kissing gate. Beyond this, bear left to follow the shoreline. Birdwatchers will be in their element as this stretch of coast is home to numerous waders, seabirds and wildfowl. Pick up a faint grassy track

25

Dun Nosebridge

Distance 2.25km **Time** 1 hour (round trip)
Terrain farm track, then path; grazing
livestock so dogs must be kept under
tight control, especially during lambing
season **Map** OS Explorer 352
Access no public transport to the start

Islay is dotted with historic relics and
this Iron Age fort is an excellent example
– a fortified earthwork mound half-
hidden amidst fertile farmland, just
waiting to be discovered. This short quiet
walk allows time to explore the ramparts
and appreciate the views of the
surrounding Islay hills.

This walk starts from Mulindry Bridge on
the unclassified back road between
Bridgend and Cluanach. In Bridgend take
the A846 Bowmore road and turn left
(signed for Cluanach) after the hotel. The
road bends and crosses the River Laggan at
Mulindry Bridge. A little further on there is

limited parking near the houses marked as
'Schoolhouse' on the OS map. Take care
not to block any access to the houses.

Begin the walk by heading back down
the road and crossing the bridge over the
river before turning right onto a farm
track. Go through the gate and keep left
when the track forks to avoid an area of
boggy ground, soon aiming right to rejoin
the original track and passing through
pleasant woodland of oak and hazel trees.
As the glen opens out, the unmistakably
man-made grassy dome of Dun
Nosebridge can be seen up ahead and
it becomes clearer why this position
was a sound strategic and defensive choice
with its extensive views across a wide
sweep of land.

Islay has 80 documented ancient forts
and Dun Nosebridge is one of the biggest.
The three-tiered ramparts are still very
evident; these would have encircled two

◀ Dun Nosebridge

deep ditches. The fort is thought to date from somewhere between 1000BC and 1000AD – it has never been excavated and an accurate date is not available. Its exact purpose is unknown, as Dun Nosebridge and other similar forts were probably built before the Viking raids on Islay, although they may well have been used to defend against later attacks. They may have been built as elaborate status symbols or to protect against inter-clan or family warfare based on land ownership and control. It is certain that people continued to live at the site well beyond the Iron Age, probably right up to the time of the Clearances on Islay in the mid-19th century.

Walk to the back of the fort and take the track around the left side before climbing to the surprisingly spacious summit. Originally a wall would have encircled this area as a final level of protection, and timber and turf buildings would have stood in the rectangular space. The commanding position, in the midst of the fertile farmland of the Upper Laggan, also offers excellent views of the main hills on Islay. Beinn Bheigier, Glas Bheinn and Sgorr nam Faoileann, with their white quartzite rock caps, provide rewarding hillwalks over challenging terrain, despite their relatively low stature.

When you have finished exploring the Dun, return to the road and bridge by the same outward route.

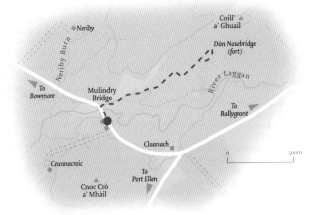

Bridgend Woods and Woollen Mill

Distance 6.5km **Time** 2 hours 30
Terrain woodland tracks and paths,
boggy in places **Map** OS Explorer 353
Access nearest bus stop is in Bridgend,
500m from the start

Once part of the grounds of Islay House,
Bridgend's woodlands now provide a
wonderful sheltered green space to
explore. Carpeted with snowdrops at the
start of the year and later a sea of
bluebells, this makes a scenic setting for
a walk, topped off with a visit to the Islay
Woollen Mill where traditional tweed
cloth is still woven.

To find the start point, drive out of
Bridgend on the A846 Port Askaig road.
At a sign for Islay House Square, turn left
and the car park for the woodland walks is
immediately on the left. The walk starts
from here, but the Square is worth
visiting – its old servants' quarters and

estate buildings now housing a number
of enterprises, including the Islay Ales
Brewery, craft galleries and an outlet for
the fruit and vegetables grown in the
productive community garden located in
the huge walled gardens that used to
service the house.

Start the walk by going through the
gate from the woodland walks car park,
crossing the main road and taking the
track into the woods between a pair of
white gateposts.

These woods were originally planted in
the early 19th century as part of a large
parkland attached to Islay House. Home
to the hereditary lairds of Islay, the
Campbells, Islay House was built in 1677
and expanded and renovated over the
next couple of centuries. In order for the
parkland to be laid out, an entire village
was demolished near the current location
of the square and the residents were

28

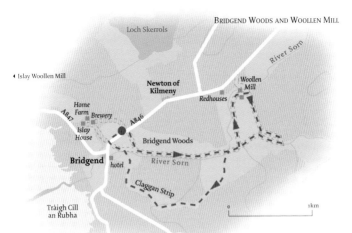

Loch Skerrols

River Sorn

◀ Islay Woollen Mill

Newton of Kilmeny

Woollen Mill

Redhouses

Home Farm
Brewery
A846

A847

Islay House

Bridgend

hotel

Bridgend Woods

River Sorn

Claggan Strip

Tràigh Cill an Rubha

0   1 km

moved to a newly expanded Bowmore.

When you reach the first junction, bear left along a track signed for Bridgend Woods. This runs alongside the River Sorn where you may spot dippers and long-tailed tits. Stay on the main track, ignoring a branch that joins from the left, and go straight ahead at the next junction, soon crossing a wooden bridge over the river. Pass a track to the right and take the next on the left signed for Waulk Mill. This winds through dense woods of elm, sycamore, beech and even some redwood trees. Take the signed path on the left to detour to the woollen mill, turning left at a track to arrive at the bridge and mill. Here cloth is still woven on traditional Victorian looms. Originally dating from 1883 it was re-opened in 1981 and you can often take a tour.

From the mill retrace your steps up the track and path on the right to return to

the main route, turning left to continue on the track. At a minor road turn right, heading downhill through farmland until you can turn right onto a track (SP Waulk Mill Circular). Cross a burn and keep left when a track joins from the right.

The next section can be very muddy; if you want to shortcut and avoid any bog, continue ahead across the bridge and retrace the outward route. Otherwise turn left for Bridgend just before the bridge and, at a break in the trees, cross to a gate to enter a narrow area of woodland known as the Claggan Strip. Here the going is rougher and there are sometimes fallen trees to clamber over. Continue ahead at a crossroads, staying on the narrow path. After a wooden bridge turn left onto a track which soon reaches the main road. Cross and continue on another track, looking out for a path on the right which runs alongside the road to get back to the start.

Ballygrant and the Lily Loch

Distance 9.5km **Time** 3 hours
Terrain tracks, good paths, shared
cyclepath at the edge of the main road
Map OS Explorer 353 **Access** bus from
Port Askaig, Bowmore and Port Ellen
to Ballygrant

This delightful circuit meanders through
the lush countryside, woodland and
fishing lochs of the Dunlossit Estate.
The walk then follows an off-road
cycletrack through the small community
of Keills for the return to Ballygrant.

Park or get off the bus in the centre of
Ballygrant on the A846 between Bridgend
and Port Askaig. You can combine this
walk with a half-day visit to Loch Finlaggan
where the ruins of the ancient Lordship of

the Isles can be explored; the visitor centre
is signed around 2km further along the
A846 towards Port Askaig.

One of the oldest villages on Islay,
Ballygrant was traditionally the centre of
the agricultural industry with a prosperous
grain mill used for milling oats, although
between the 1600s and 1800s many
residents worked in the local silver and
lead mines. The walk starts by heading
south along the minor road signed for
Mulindry, just north (towards Port Askaig)
of the parking area in Ballygrant. This
passes the village hall; when the road forks
bear left to pass a speed restriction sign.

Soon turn left through a farm gate to
head along a woodland track which is part
of the Dunlossit Estate, one of five main

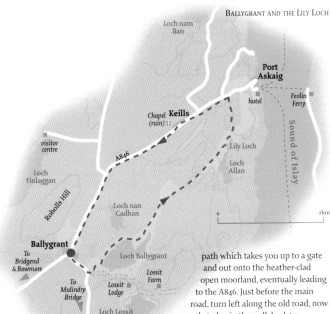

estates that own much of Islay. Pass a farm building to shortly reach Loch Ballygrant. Turn left here to follow the shoreside track. The loch is home to a variety of birds and is a popular fishing spot. The remains of an Iron Age crannog can usually be seen poking out of the water. Stay on the track, ignoring a turning to the left, and soon leave the water for a straight section of track before arriving at the Lily Loch. Named for the waterlilies which cover almost every inch of the water's surface in summer, it's a lovely place for a break with picnic tables at the far end.

Turn left opposite the picnic tables onto a path which takes you up to a gate and out onto the heather-clad open moorland, eventually leading to the A846. Just before the main road, turn left along the old road, now a path, to begin the walk back to Ballygrant. The path runs parallel to the current A846, but is mostly shielded by a wall. At the village of Keills cross to the other side of the road to follow the pavement through the village. The name derives from the Gaelic Cill, meaning 'church', and the ruins of a chapel attributed to St Columba can be found in the graveyard here. Much later, flax was grown in the area around the village and many of the present-day cottages were built to house weavers brought in from Glasgow.

At the far end of the village cross back to the south side of the road to once again pick up a path running parallel to it; follow this for around 3km back to Ballygrant.

Rhuvaal Lighthouse

Distance 13.5km **Time** 5 hours (round trip)
Terrain grassy track, very boggy and can
be hard to follow in places
Map OS Explorer 353 **Access** no public
transport to the start

This out-and-back route takes you from
Bunnahabhain Distillery to the most
northerly point on Islay where you'll find
Rubha a' Mhail (or Rhuvaal) Lighthouse.
Crossing rough and challenging open
country for much of the distance, the
route gives lovely views over the water to
Jura, Colonsay and even Mull on
a clear day.

Bunnahabhain is a settlement
built around the distillery which
dates from 1881. The distillery,
like most on Islay, runs a full
schedule of tours, although
booking in advance is advisable.
Its more remote setting makes it
an atmospheric one to visit. Its
name is from the Gaelic,
meaning 'Mouth of the River' –
referring to the Margadale River

which supplies water to the distillery and
runs out into the Sound of Islay just north
of the buildings. Before reaching the main
distillery buildings, just before the road
descends, there is a parking area on a
grassy triangle on the left.

Start the walk by taking the track inland
from here. You shortly go through a gate
and turn right immediately to pass a
concrete sheep fank and reach another
gate. This leads to a track which drops
downhill into trees. At a fork keep left to
cross a footbridge over the river. On the far
side the track grows much
fainter; it is hard to follow in places as the
terrain gets rougher and boggy. The route
sticks close to a line of telegraph poles
before heading further inland to avoid
some steep ravines. In summer high
bracken can sometimes obscure the track,
but it is usually clear enough here, soon
fording a small burn. Across the straits is
a direct view of the scree-girt Paps of Jura,
though they can be shrouded in cloud
even when the rest of the skies are clear.

Keep an eye (and nose) out for the

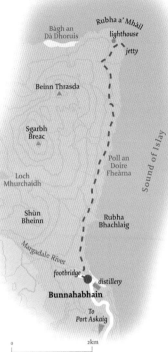

wild goats that frequent this area, often venturing down to the shoreline to eat the seaweed. There are also red deer here, although far fewer than on Jura where they outnumber the human population by around 30 to one.

Now and again the very tip of Rhuvaal Lighthouse comes into view. Much further on, the track descends steeply to cross another burn before rising and bending left and then aiming directly for the lighthouse buildings. Designed by David and Thomas from the famous lighthouse-building Stevenson family, it was constructed from brick in 1859 and stands 36m tall. Now fully automated, there once would have been several lighthouse keepers and their families stationed in the cottages below the light. The buildings and garden area are private and not accessible to the public.

When you get to the small supply track linking the jetty and lighthouse bear right to descend to the jetty, passing an old stone-built store on the way. The jetty is a great place to enjoy the views out to Colonsay, with Mull beyond, as well as watching for seals, otters and passing seabirds. The elevated trig point just behind the store building provides an even better vantage point.

The return route is by the same outward track, the views of Bunnahabhain improving all the time and maybe tempting you to reward yourself with a dram. For a far longer and much more

strenuous linear walk it is possible to instead carry on along the coast to round the pathless headland beyond the lighthouse, crossing a stunning beach at Bàgh an Da Dhoruis and continuing over very rough ground with a number of caves and sea arches to eventually reach a track and then the road near Killinallan Point. You would need to have arranged transport from here.

Killinallan Point

Distance **10.5 km** Time **3 hours 30**
Terrain **sandy beach, track through fields
with livestock (keep dogs under control);
if it is high tide when you arrive you may
prefer to do the walk the opposite way
round** Map **OS Explorer 353**
Access **no public transport to the start**

**Killinallan Point lies opposite Ardnave
Point across the tidal waters of Loch
Gruinart, popular with seabirds, waders,
geese and seals. This very fine walk takes
in the sandy beach and dunes, revealing
views across the sea to Colonsay.**

To reach the start, take the signed road
towards Killinallan from the B8017, just
east of the RSPB visitor centre at Gruinart.
The road is rough; just before a gate there
is parking on the turf on the left side –

well before the farm at Killinallan itself.
Begin by heading to the shore via a gate
waymarked with a white arrow. At low
tide seals gather on the sandbanks
opposite; this is a good place from which
to watch them as they are unfazed by
people when they are safely on the other
side of the water.

Aim right to walk northwards towards
the headland – taking care at low tide as
some of the sands can be very soft.
Wading birds congregate here and you
will also see the exposed cages in which
oysters are grown commercially. As winter
approaches these sands and the nearby
dunes are a fantastic place to watch the
arrival of thousands of geese that
overwinter on Loch Gruinart. Round the
headland to walk across the light sand of

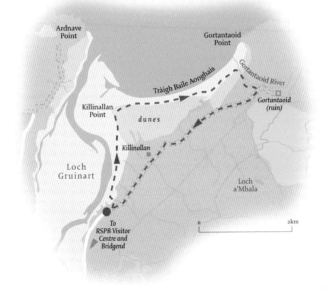

◀ Ruin at Killinallan

Traigh Baile Aonghais. Further on, a burn has to be crossed; this is usually fairly easy, but if the water level is high it may be necessary to take the small path inland to reach the track for a safe crossing. Continuing along the sand, you eventually reach the Gortantaoid River. Just before the water take a faint path leading up through the dunes, keeping high above the river before aiming slightly to the right to reach a gate. Once past the gate you can head over to the left to return to the river and view the waterfall before continuing on the faint path, aiming southeast to hit a farm track.

Here the ruins of Gortantaoid Farm can be found, with rhubarb plants still thriving in the remains of the kitchen garden. Turn right to follow the track, passing through a couple of gates on the approach to Killinallan Farm which is still worked. Keep straight on, passing through two more gates before the track returns to the parking area at the start.

Ardnave Point

Gortantaoid Point

Gortantaoid River

Traigh Baile Aonghais

Killinallan Point

dunes

Gortantaoid (ruin)

Killinallan

Loch Gruinart

Loch a'Mhala

0   2km

To RSPB Visitor Centre and Bridgend

The Rhinns of Islay is the name given to the large peninsula that makes up the westernmost part of the island. The main settlements are the picturesque whitewashed fishing villages of Port Charlotte and Portnahaven, both well worth exploring on foot. The area also boasts great beaches – from the wide sandy bays of Machir and Saligo to the more intimate coves waiting to be explored from Sanaigmore. Designated as a special protection area, the Rhinns are home to a large number of overwintering geese and birds that descend on the area annually. Loch Gruinart is an RSPB reserve and a great introduction to Islay's unique birdlife. Trails lead to excellent hides overlooking the reserve, whilst those seeking out the rare chough or happy to watch the ever-present seals lounging around on sandbanks should head to nearby Ardnave Point.

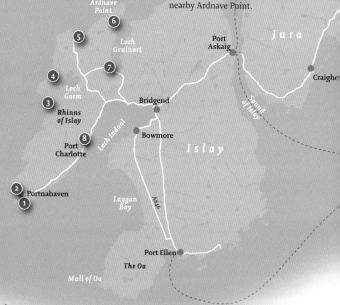

The Rhinns of Islay

Port Wemyss and Portnahaven

Distance 2.5km Time 1 hour
Terrain minor roads and surfaced paths
Map OS Explorer 353 Access bus from
Bowmore to Portnahaven

The twin coastal villages of Portnahaven
and Port Wemyss are among the most
picturesque on Islay. This exploration on
foot gives you the chance to meander
around the cottages and visit the church
and sandy anchorage, as well as taking in
the sea views and hopefully spotting a
seal or two. There is a seasonal café in
Port Wemyss and a well-regarded
restaurant and bar in Portnahaven.

If driving, the walk starts from a parking
area between Portnahaven and Port
Wemyss, although if you have arrived by
bus you can pick up the circuit anywhere
in Portnahaven. To reach the parking area
when driving into the village from Port
Charlotte, turn left off the A847 just after
the speed limit sign, passing the old

school to reach Port Wemyss. Turn right
and, after leaving the houses behind, the
parking area is ahead, where the road
bends to the right.

The walk starts by returning along the
road towards the cottages of Port Wemyss.
Both villages were built to accommodate
tenants who were cleared from Islay's
interior during the 1830s. Port Wemyss
was built by Walter Frederick Campbell;
Campbell also founded Port Ellen which
he named after his wife and Port
Charlotte, named for his mother. Port
Wemyss was originally called
Wemysshaven after his father-in-law, the
8th Earl of Wemyss.

Dominating the view to the sea and the
island of Orsay are the Rhinns of Islay
Lighthouse, built by Robert Stevenson of
the famous lighthouse-building family in
1825. Some 131 steps spiral up to the top
of the tower and the light can be seen
across the water for 24 nautical miles.

◀ Portnahaven

Before being converted to electric in 1978, a team of lighthouse keepers housed on Orsay kept the light going throughout the night. The lighthouse was fully automated in 1996.

Opposite Burnside Lodge – which operates as a café in summer – turn right onto the fisherman's coastal path, winding around the shore below the village. Common seals are frequent visitors to the waters here and there have been reports of summer visits by dolphins and even basking sharks. You may also see gannets diving into the sea to follow shoals of fish. At a path junction bear right to head downhill, and then keep left to stay on the coastal path which eventually leads up to the southern end of the village. Turn right along the road, then right again to follow the road out of the village, passing the old school and then reaching the A847.

Turn left to approach Portnahaven, passing the community hall and keeping straight ahead at the junction to reach a wonderful vantage point over the sandy bay and harbour at the heart of the village. The church on the right is worth a quick visit. Built in 1828, it was one of a number of 'parliamentary churches' built by a grant to increase the number of churches in rural areas. It is a classic Thomas Telford T-shaped design, with three upstairs galleries of pews facing the pulpit, in addition to the downstairs seating. The two entrances were said to have been designed for use by parishioners from Portnahaven and Port Wemyss respectively and the interior would have allowed the communities to remain segregated.

Continue downhill past the pretty village cottages and the An Tigh Seinnse pub and restaurant where you turn left to pass in front of the houses facing the sea. Beyond the post office turn right to pass the cottages on the far side of the bay. A small gate at the end of the street leads to a rough path linking to the lane which gives access to the jetty. Turn left onto the lane to return to the parking area.

Portnahaven beachcomber

Distance 6.5km **Time** 2 hours 30
Terrain rough coastal path, indistinct in
places **Map** OS Explorer 353 **Access** bus
from Bowmore to Portnahaven

**Explore the intricate wild coastline north
of the pretty village of Portnahaven. The
rocky shoreline is a haven for wildlife,
especially seals, and this route visits
both a sandy cove and a pebbly beach.**

The start point is the southern end of
Portnahaven where there is a parking
area, but the route also loops around the
back of the harbour near the bus stop and
you can start from there if arriving by bus.

To reach the parking area when driving
into the village from Port Charlotte, turn
left off the A847 just after the speed limit
sign, passing the old school to reach Port
Wemyss. Turn right and, after leaving the
houses behind, the parking area is ahead,
where the road bends to the right. From

here, walk north along the road to reach
the east side of the sandy anchorage in
the middle of Portnahaven. At the public
toilets fork left to head along the west
side of the harbour, passing the small
post office.

Follow the road as it curves to the right
and pass the front of the An Tigh Seinnse
pub which is popular for seafood or for a
drink. After the last house take the path
on the left to cross the turf behind the
shoreline, passing between a fence and a
wall and bearing right to climb a stile.
Here the faint path picks its way across a
mixture of rock and grass with the island
of Eilean Mhic Coinnich just offshore.
This is a favourite haunt of the seals in
this area and you are likely to see them
bobbing about in the water; you may hear
their haunting song if they are basking on
the island rocks.

Eventually you reach a pebbly beach

with the path meandering to find the easiest course across the rocks, passing through a gate in the fence halfway across. Keep to the left of the house at the far side of the bay before steering right to emerge on the minor road. Bear left onto the road which climbs past a number of houses until it comes to a grassy parking area beside a house. The small gate ahead is signed for the sands; go through it and descend the steep path to reach a perfectly formed sandy beach.

At the far side of the beach a vague path climbs steeply up the grassy slope at the back of the sand. Aim right to a gate and turn right on the track to detour inland around the experimental wave-energy power station. Go through the first gate on the left and turn left to follow the fence back towards the coast. After going through a gap in the fence, turn right to run alongside the fence and, beyond another gap in the fence, the faint path continues around the back of a deep sea inlet.

The next section is delightful if pathless. Keep following the coast, keeping well above the inlets and headland. Once on the north side of the headland of Rubha na Faing the route is forced inland by a deep inlet which is another popular place for seals. At the

back of the inlet cross a stile and then aim uphill towards a gap in an old stone wall. Bear left to go through the gap and follow the fence ahead to a gate leading to the minor road. Turn right to begin the return to Portnahaven. At the house above the sandy beach the outward route via the pebble-filled bay can be taken or you can stay on the quiet back road, turning right at a T-junction to return to the start.

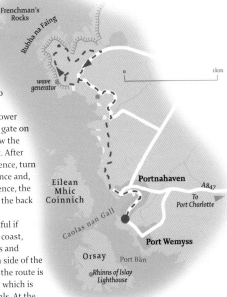

Machir Bay

Distance 3km **Time** 1 hour
Terrain grassy track and sandy beach
Map OS Explorer 353 **Access** no public
transport to the start

**Explore the spectacular sweep of
white sands at Machir Bay on this
straightforward walk. Allow time to see
the beautiful carved Celtic cross in the
graveyard and maybe sample a dram (or
coffee) at Islay's youngest distillery,
Kilchoman, near the start of the route.**

Machir Bay is in the far northwest of
Islay; take the B8018 from the Bowmore to
Port Charlotte road and carry on following
the signs for Kilchoman, eventually
continuing towards the bay along a track
at the end of the public road to reach a
parking area.

The walk starts by going through the
gate beside the information board and

heading along the track set well back from
the dunes. After passing a boggy hollow
on the inland side, the track narrows to
become a path. The name of the bay
derives from the sandy coastal grassland,
or machair, which becomes a mass of
flowering plants in spring and early
summer. After some time, the southern
end of Machir Bay comes into view.

Follow the path to a gate and stile on
the right and, after climbing this, aim
down towards the beach. The ongoing
path eventually leads to Kilchiaran and
would make a lovely walk in itself,
especially if transport could be arranged.

However, this walk is all about the sea
and sand. Machir Bay boasts more than
2km of pristine sand and its waves often
attract skilled surfers, although the water
here is dangerous for swimming due to
strong rip tides. Return northwards along

◀ Machir Bay

the beach for just over 1km, before aiming inland to reach an obvious break in the dunes. Once through the dunes there is a clear path that leads back to the parking area.

Before leaving the area, don't miss the churchyard at Kilchoman where there is a fine carved cross, as well as some interesting gravestones; and you can also walk a little further to see the military cemetery. To reach the churchyard you can either walk back up the road and turn right for Kilchoman or there is limited parking near the now ruined church. It is thought this site was home to a very early Christian chapel which was replaced in the 1300s by a medieval church; in turn this was replaced in 1827 by the more modern ruined structure that stands today. Depopulation of the area meant that by 1977 the church had ceased to be used and has since fallen into disrepair. The carvings on the large standing cross have fared much better and images of the crucifixion, angels and a horse and rider can clearly be made out.

The cross dates from the 1300s or 1400s and is one of a number on Islay carved in the Iona style. There are also a number of flat grave slabs with impressive carved images of knights or priests that are worth seeking out.

The military cemetery stands alone, closer to the bay. Here lie the graves of 71 British servicemen who lost their lives when the *HMS Otranto* collided with another ship in the bay in bad weather in 1918. Originally the 351 American servicemen who also died in the tragedy were buried here before being repatriated to America. The *Otranto* disaster is one of two ship losses commemorated by the American Monument on the Oa which you can also walk to (see page 14).

43

Saligo Bay

Distance 5.5km Time 2 hours 30
Terrain coastal path and beach; grazing
sheep, dogs to be kept under tight
control Map OS Explorer 353
Access no public transport to the start

This figure-of-eight walk explores the
stunning coastline either side of sandy
Saligo Bay, taking in a natural arch and
the small often deserted beach of Traigh
Fleisgein Bheag.

To reach the minor road leading to
Saligo Bay take the B8018 towards
Sanaigmore and turn left after the
phonebox at Carnduncan. After skirting
around Loch Gorm, there is limited
parking near the Saligo River. Regular
access is needed to the fields, so take care
not to block entrances and also keep
passing places clear.

The walk starts by going through the
gate past the 'Welcome to Saligo' sign. As
there are sheep grazing on this
unenclosed land, the farmer requests that
dogs are not taken during the lambing
season (April to June) and are kept under
tight control at other times. The concrete
ruins are the remains of a Second World
War radar station – one of a string of
coastal stations built around the UK
during the conflict to give an early
warning of incoming enemy aircraft. After
a short distance along the track, fork left
onto a path which heads through the
dunes onto the beach.

Saligo is one of the best beaches on
Islay, renowned for its fine sand, surf and
spectacular sunsets. It's a lovely place to
while away a few hours, though
swimming is not recommended because

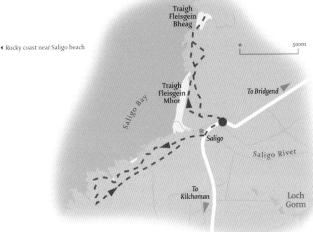

Traigh
Fleisgein
Bheag

Traigh
Fleisgein
Mhor

Saligo Bay

To Bridgend

Saligo

Saligo River

To
Kilchoman

Loch
Gorm

500m

◄ Rocky coast near Saligo beach

of the strong currents. Bear right across the sands to reach the far end of the beach and then aim right to pick up a grassy track. Turn left along this track, which eventually leads to the small hidden sandy beach, Traigh Fleisgein Bheag. The eagle-eyed may be able to find a couple of small crude gravestones standing just to the north of the bay, one inscribed with the date 1818. It is thought that these may belong to drowned sailors as they were often buried looking out to sea rather than being interred in the local graveyard.

Behind this small beach take the grassy track which soon bears right and returns to the gate at the start of the walk. For the second section, which is rougher, turn right along the road from the gate, crossing the Saligo River and thereby avoiding a paddle on the sands. Just beyond the cottage on the right, turn right through the small gate and cross the

field, aiming for the gateway leading through the stone wall. The route now continues along the coast, taking in a variety of deep inlets and sea-sculpted rocks. The signs of otters can be seen here so a stop and a patient scan with the binoculars may be rewarded with a sighting. In places the ground can be boggy underfoot, but generally the going is good.

When you reach a fence, head inland to get a view of the impressive natural arches spanning the deep geo or inlet. This is also a good area for watching seabirds. Return via the outward coastal route, retracing your steps to the stone wall and then the cottage. If you need to get back in more haste, a faint track running along the bottom of the raised beach below the inland cliffs will also bring you back to the start.

Sights and sands of Sanaigmore

Distance 4.5km **Time** 2 hours
Terrain coastal path, rough optional
descent to a second beach; livestock
present, so keep dogs under tight control
Map OS Explorer 353 **Access** no public
transport to the start

Explore three contrasting beaches: a
small pebbly bay popular with wildlife,
a wide arc of sand and a hidden sheltered
cove – an idyllic spot to while away a
sunny afternoon. Sanaigmore is also
home to the Outback Art Gallery and
small café.

To reach the start take the B8018 from
the Bowmore to Port Charlotte road and
follow it along its tortuous length to the
road end at Sanaigmore. Before you reach
the gallery and farm buildings there is

parking available adjacent to the large
memorial. The waters off the Islay coast
are treacherous; this memorial
commemorates the 241 Irish emigrants
who perished when their boat, *The
Exmouth*, was wrecked near here in 1847.
The bodies of 108 – many of them
women and children – were recovered and
buried nearby.

Walk past the farm buildings and
gallery, keeping straight on when the
track forks and passes the agricultural
sheds. Go through a clear but narrow gap
in the stone wall and follow the wall to
the right before reaching a grassy track,
then turn left along this. The track leads
through a gateway and then out onto the
springy turf at the back of Sanaigmore
Bay. Stay on the track until it fords a burn,

then aim left towards the sea and a small pebbled bay. Popular with seabirds and seals this is a good place for a break and a spot of wildlife watching.

Head back towards Sanaigmore by crossing the back of this small bay and the headland, aiming in the direction of the farmhouse buildings. Once across the grassy headland, stay on the left side of the fence to reach a gate which you go through to access the beach at Sanaigmore Bay. Walk across the sand to the far end of the bay and then follow a very faint path up onto the grass. This path now stays near the edge of the coast, winding between small rocky knolls over rough and sometimes boggy ground.

Your reward is a fantastic view of the hidden beach, Port Ghille Greamhair, which sits in a deep inlet forming a natural windbreak. The route down to the beach itself is fairly rough; to find the start of the narrow path keep following the cliffs inland until parallel with the back of the sand - from here the route winds down the cliff. For an easier but longer approach, keep walking inland until level with the beach and then aim directly for the sands.

To return, walk back up from the beach and retrace the outward route along the cliff for a short distance before joining a faint track which runs parallel to the coast and emerges at a gate near the memorial.

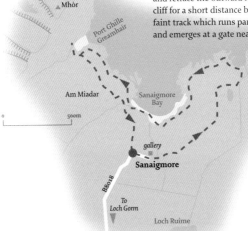

Ardnave Point

Distance 6km **Time** 3 hours
Terrain grassy track, pathless section with
minimal waymarkers, dogs should be
kept under tight control due to
groundnesting birds and livestock
Map OS Explorer 353 **Access** no public
transport to the start

This walk offers a bit of everything:
stunning coastal scenery, dunes and deep
inlets, views to Jura, Mull and Colonsay,
the remains of a roundhouse dating from
2000BC, and a wide variety of wildlife
throughout the year.

Keen birdwatchers descend on Ardnave
to spot large flocks of the rare chough, one
of the species for which Islay is best
known. During the autumn grey seals pup
on an offshore island. Cattle and sheep
graze on the unfenced headland which is
also home to groundnesting birds, so any
dogs should be kept under close control.

To reach Ardnave take the B8017 from
the Bowmore to Port Charlotte road; turn

onto a minor road by the RSPB Loch
Gruinart Visitor Centre at Aoradh Farm to
head north. There is a grassy parking area
at the north end of Ardnave Loch, just
after the cattle grid. The loch itself is the
winter home of whooper swans, wigeon,
and geese which arrive after a long
migration from the Arctic.

Start by walking away from the loch
along a sandy track, past an information
board. Instead of going straight on through
the farm gate, turn right to remain on the
main track which follows the western
shores of Loch Gruinart. At low tide there
are often seals hauled out on the
sandbanks safely surrounded by water.

Choughs are the main draw for
birdwatchers here. A member of the crow
family, choughs have the familiar black
body but with bright red legs and beak.
The RSPB estimates there are fewer than
300 breeding pairs in all of Britain and
Ardnave Point is home to a fair
proportion of them. They attract attention

with sweeping acrobatic flights and in the autumn and winter are often seen flying in sizeable flocks.

A kissing gate leads onto another section of sandy track which gradually narrows and becomes less distinct. There are occasional waymarkers, though the route keeps well to the left of the first signpost and then reaches the second one at another kissing gate further north. From this point you can climb up to the highest dunes for far-reaching views over Ardnave Point. The island ahead is Nave Island, home to a maternity ward of pupping grey seals in the autumn. Further afield, on a clear day, the islands of Colonsay and Jura are visible.

Go through the kissing gate and up and over the dunes to reach the site of an ancient roundhouse. It is thought to date from around 2000BC which would make it either Neolithic or very early Bronze Age. Although not much remains visible today beyond a mound of stones, when it was excavated in the 1980s pottery and a variety of stone tools were discovered.

The next section crosses pathless ground. Aim WSW, keeping parallel with the coast to reach a kissing gate in a fence about 300m inland. The route now follows a sandy track round the west coast of the peninsula. Cattle usually graze in this area, so keep a sensible distance if they have calves or especially if you have a dog. Farm buildings soon come into view ahead; at this point go through a gate towards the farm. Follow the signs, turning left to pass a metal shed and then bearing right along a stone-walled track, passing the large farmhouse. As you skirt along Loch Ardnave on the way back to the parking area look out for the remains of a crannog – a man-made island – near the far bank.

Map labels:
Nave Island
Ardnave Point
Eilean Beag
Cnoc na Faire
Tràigh Nòstaig
dunes
dunes
Ardnave
Loch Gruinart
Ardnave Loch
To RSPB Visitor Centre and Bridgend
0   1km

◀ Track through the dunes

Loch Gruinart

Distance 2.5km **Time** 1 hour (leave extra time for the bird hides)
Terrain clear and easy waymarked paths
Map OS Explorer 353 **Access** no public transport to the start

Islay is a birdwatcher's paradise and this walk visiting two hides on the RSPB's Loch Gruinart Reserve is a great introduction, accessible to all the family. The reserve is the winter home of thousands of barnacle and white-fronted geese, and in summer offers the chance to spot corncrakes, hen harriers and peregrine falcons. Whatever the time of year, your visit is likely to be rewarded with a mix of wildlife due to the rich and varied habitat of the grassland and open water that makes up the reserve.

To reach the car park, head north towards Ardnave from the RSPB Loch Gruinart Visitor Centre at Aoradh Farm, located on the B8017. The visitor centre is itself worth a visit, especially if this is your first time on Islay or if you want to check what birds have been spotted recently. From the car park on the left-hand side of the Ardnave road, walk back through the gate and turn right along the road briefly before going through a gate on the far side. At the first junction keep straight ahead to reach the viewing platform overlooking the waters of Loch Gruinart. You may get your first glimpse of the geese from here, as well as an appreciation of the special landscape and habitat that the RSPB are conserving.

Continue on the path which leads down

to a gate. Bear left onto a track and then turn right onto a path waymarked with white arrows. Keeping left you'll soon reach the first hide. Many of the birds here are seasonal and a book records recent sightings. The spring is usually a hive of activity with wading birds including redshank, curlew, snipe and lapwing. If you keep your binoculars scanning the water you may even be lucky enough to spot an otter.

From the hide return to the track and up past the viewing platform. This time turn right at the junction to follow the signed Woodland Trail. A section of boardwalk keeps the path off boggy ground. It then winds through a thicket of trees popular with smaller birds. Once you reach the more open ground you are in corncrake territory. Notoriously difficult to spot, the birds arrive from Africa in mid-May and tend to favour the dense patches of flag iris or nettles that dot the island. You are much more likely to hear their loud rasping call which is quite unmistakable. The RSPB organise evening walks to try and spot them. When the path joins

another, keep to the right, aiming downhill and out of the woods towards the waters of Loch Gruinart and the second hide. Barn owls, hen harriers, golden eagles and even the occasional osprey stopping off on its migration to Africa have been spotted hunting here. When you have finished bird-spotting, return to the tree cover and keep on the waymarked main path to head uphill before it emerges on the road. Turn left for a short road walk back to the car park.

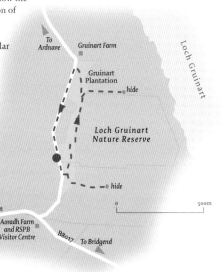

◀ Looking towards Loch Gruinart

Port Charlotte explorer

Distance 5km **Time** 2 hours **Terrain** paths (sometimes muddy), minor roads, livestock in fields (keep dogs under tight control) **Map** OS Explorer 353
Access bus from Port Ellen, Port Askaig and Bowmore to Port Charlotte

Port Charlotte grew up as a distillery village, its picturesque whitewashed cottages built to house the workers. This walk climbs across pleasant farmland to look down on the cottages and coastline. Leave time to explore the village where there is a hotel and café, as well as the engaging Museum of Islay Life.

There is usually on-street parking in the centre of Port Charlotte. Start from outside the Port Charlotte Hotel on the main road and head north, passing the hotel garden and the youth hostel, which is housed in one of the warehouse buildings that once formed part of the Lochindaal Distillery. There are plans by neighbouring Bruichladdich Distillery (once seen as the young upstart in the distilling world but now part of giant Rémy Cointreau) to reopen the distillery here.

After the bridge you can visit the Museum of Islay Life on the left. Along with the usual collection of crofting implements and household possessions, the museum holds a fascinating collection of human interest stories and items that really tell the often tragic history of the

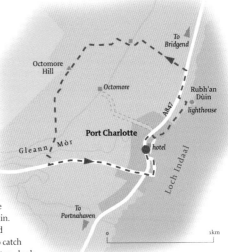

To
Bridgend

Octomore
Hill

Octomore

Rubh'an
Dùin

lighthouse

A847

Port Charlotte

hotel

Gleann Mòr

Loch Indaal

To
Portnahaven

0   1km

island, adding a lot of background interest to the places you visit during a holiday.

Pass the café and turn right through the car park (reserved for the café and medical centre only) to take the signed path down to the shoreline. Aim left, staying close to the fence and going through a gate to head towards the lighthouse at Rubh'an Duin. This coastal path is a good place for the eagle-eyed to catch sight of an otter in the water – look for the telltale V-shape wave which is formed as it moves through the water. Keep straight on through a gate near a house and, as you approach the lighthouse, bear left inland – aiming for the gate at the corner of the field. After the gate turn right and follow the road until just after the bungalow, where you turn left. This track leads uphill before curving left; you now go through a gate to pass a lonely house with good views of the coast below. Pass to the left of the house and go up through the farm gate, aiming left to cross the field on a diagonal and reach a gate sited halfway along the fence.

Once through the gate aim for the top of the hill, passing just to the left of the forestry. Here you can enjoy sweeping views over Port Charlotte, Loch Indaal and Bowmore beyond. Pass through a gateway in the next fence, keeping straight on as you bear southwest to find a gate in the stone wall. Carry straight on, downhill, keeping on the right-hand side of the wall. The area at the bottom where you need to cross the burn that flows through Gleann Mor can be boggy at times, so pick your route with care. Eventually the walk reaches a farm gate and joins the minor road just below the waterworks.

Turn left here to follow the road down to Port Charlotte. At the main road a left turn returns you directly to the hotel; otherwise continue ahead to explore the pier and shore on a slightly longer variation.

Jura contrasts markedly with its near neighbour Islay. Stark, wild and elemental, it stretches for 48km and is 11km wide, but has fewer than 200 residents – said to be outnumbered 30 to 1 by red deer. Most visitors arrive on the short vehicular ferry from Port Askaig and then proceed by bus or car to the main settlement of Craighouse, 16km along the relatively sylvan east coast which contrasts with the hills and moors that make up most of the island. Home to Jura's distillery, Craighouse also boasts a school, well-stocked community shop, café, hotel and sheltered anchorage in the picturesque bay which brings an itinerant community of yachties to the island.

The steep quartzite domes of the three Paps lie at the heart of the island and dominate its landscape. The highest, Beinn an Oir, rises to 785m from sea-level moorland and the tough, stony climb is rewarded with breathtaking views over sea, islands and the mainland.

Jura is home to a wide variety of wildlife, including golden eagles, hen harriers, otters, wild goats, seals and the occasional passing minke whale or orca. Many of the shorter walks take in particularly good wildlife-watching spots, as well as sandy beaches and a remote bothy. Reaching the northern end of the island is a tough hike, ending at cliffs overlooking the notorious Corryvreckan whirlpool and passing Barnhill – the remote retreat where George Orwell wrote 1984.

Jura

Whitefarland Bay

Distance 3.5km Time 1 hour
Terrain track, shoreline path, rough in
places Map OS Explorer 355
Access ferry from Port Askaig; bus from
Craighouse to Feolin

This is the perfect waterside stroll for
those who are only visiting Jura for a
short time – watch the tiny vehicle ferry
plying across the Sound of Islay, or look
for otters and seabirds amongst the kelp
in the shallows.

For those stepping off the ferry from
Port Askaig the route starts just to the
right along the road. Otherwise there is
parking near the slipway behind the
toilet building. Take the road towards
Craighouse (it's the only road!) and then
turn left at the old ferrymaster's house
(marked as Feolin Centre on some maps).
The track, signed for the Inver Estate,
soon doubles back on itself to head north
above the coast.

Jura used to have a direct vehicle ferry
route connecting Lagg with mainland
Kintyre which ran until the 1980s.
However, once this was decommissioned
the route via Islay became the only ferry
serving Jura until the summer passenger
ferry from Craighouse started in 2008. The
Port Askaig ferry has only been a roll-on-
roll-off boat since the 1970s; before then
any large goods or vehicles would have
arrived swinging off an unloading hook.

The track stays parallel to the shore,
providing good views to the Paps of Jura
to the right. There is some controversy
about whether these three rounded scree-
clad lumps provide the origin of the name
for the island. Some say the name Jura
(*Diura* in Gaelic) comes from the Norse for
'Udder Island', reflecting the shape of the
mountains, and some say it originates
from the Norse for 'Deer Island', given the
high number of deer. A third option
suggests it is a blend of Gaelic and Norse,

◀ Jura ferry heading to Port Askaig

meaning 'Doraid's Island'. Whatever the truth, spend a little time on Jura and you cannot fail to see numerous deer, usually against a backdrop of the Paps as they are visible from most parts of the island unless shrouded in cloud.

After about 1.5km Inver Cottage can be seen ahead and the track leads down to the shoreline. Before you reach the water, turn sharp left to head back along a coast path which stays above the pebbly shoreline at first. On the far side of the water there is a good view to the Caol Ila Distillery, with Bunnahabhain also visible further north. Look out for the telltale piles of white spraint which show that an otter has been marking its territory. If you're lucky you may catch sight of one swimming – watch for a clear V-shape in the water – or fishing amidst the kelp in the shallows. There are also a number of wading and seabirds around here, including curlew, oystercatchers, shags, grebes and sandpipers, as well as the odd gannet passing through.

Further on, the path follows the shore for short sections. These can be impassable during very high tides; if so it is necessary to head slightly inland to return on the track. In a couple of places follow the old track slightly back from the water to skirt round rocks blocking the beach route. Once nearly back to the ferry slipway the track forks; either route leads back to the start.

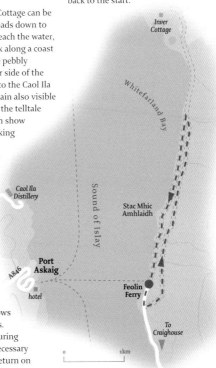

Market Loch

Distance **5km** Time **2 hours 30 (round trip)**
Terrain **track, rough path, boggy in
places, exposed steep drop above gorge**
Map **OS Explorer 355** Access **1km walk
from Craighouse to the start; bus from
Feolin to Inverlussa passes the start**

**If you want to find out where the Jura
Distillery gets the water for the two
million litres of whisky it produces each
year, take this short hike up the hillside
behind Craighouse to the peaceful shores
of Market Loch.**

Just over 1km south of Craighouse on
the A846, the main road that snakes up
the east coast of Jura (the southern
section was built by Thomas Telford in
1777), there is a parking area and a
fingerpost pointing to Market Loch. Start

by following the track away from the road,
soon passing through a gate.

At a fork, keep left. Here, if the bracken
is not too high, you will be able to see a
prehistoric standing stone on the left,
with another two smaller stones nearby.
The track leads towards the thick forestry
plantation ahead but, just before you
reach the trees, turn right onto a path that
climbs uphill. At first this follows a fence
and then runs along the edge of the high
cliff above the Allt Carragh a' Ghlinne.
Care is needed in places as the drop is
unprotected and very steep, although
there are good views down to the
tumbling water below.

Soon a waterfall comes into view, just a
little way further up the burn. Go through
a gate and continue up across the open

moorland. Here the path can be very damp underfoot. When you reach the remains of a drystone wall, follow it on the right-hand side.

Eventually you come to Loch a' Bhaile Mhargaidh. Stretching for almost 2km, the loch is known as the Market Loch locally. It has a thriving population of wild trout, as well as some brown trout hybrids introduced for fishing by the Ardfin Estate. The loch was dammed to provide a constant water supply for the Isle of Jura Distillery, as well as some properties in Craighouse. The small dam is a good place to sit and enjoy the tranquillity of the water; it is also possible to walk sections of the lochside from the dam, although the going is rough and boggy. To return to the start retrace the route back downhill.

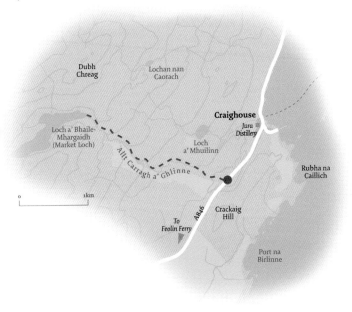

Keils and Kilearnadil Cemetery

Distance 4.75km **Time** 1 hour 30
Terrain minor roads and track
Map OS Explorer 355 **Access** bus from
Feolin to Craighouse

**This easy ramble explores the tiny
crofting community of Keils, above
Craighouse, before visiting the island's
main cemetery which contains some
fine old carved gravestones. A lovely walk
for an evening to watch the sun setting
over the bay or to sober up after a tour of
the distillery.**

Craighouse is Jura's community hub,
home to most of the island's 200-plus
residents and boasting a school, shop, café,
hotel and the distillery. There is a parking
area on the front next to the community
hall, just along from the shop. Start the
walk by heading northwards along the
road which hugs the coast. The Bay of
Small Isles, named for the ring of islands
protecting it from the wider sea and
providing safe anchorage, is a good place
to spot herons, swans and various species
of duck, as well as keeping an eye out for
the elusive otter.

The row of low terraced cottages on the
left were built for mariners. You soon pass
Craighouse Parish Church near the end of
the village. Keep going for a short distance
until you come to a left turn signed for the
cemetery. This rises gently through the
remains of the old settlement of Keils. In
1841 there were 22 houses in this small area
with a population of 102. Along with the
rest of Jura, the population declined from a
high point of around 1300 in the 1830s,
with famine, lack of employment,
industrialisation elsewhere offering paid

◄ Craighouse

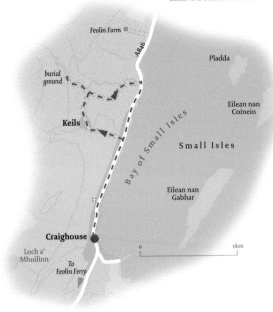

work, and some Clearances causing people to move to the mainland or emigrate and seek their fortune in the New Worlds.

Nowadays Keils is typical of many of these settlements; some new families have moved in and crofting is combined with a mixture of local work, fishing, home working and tourism to provide a living. Keep following the road; at the sharp left turn take note of the unsurfaced track on the right which will be the return route.

The road climbs and, just beyond the final house, reaches a metal gate designed to keep deer out of the cemetery. Go through it and follow the track to the right

to soon reach the graveyard. The cemetery has been enlarged and the steps lead up to the most recent part. Beyond this is the ancient burial ground; keep an eye out for the carved medieval slabs decorated with swords and Celtic designs. At the far end of the cemetery is the Campbell Mausoleum which houses the remains of the island's former lairds.

To return to Craighouse, walk back down through the gate and at the bottom of the lane take the track ahead, aiming towards the bay. This brings you out on the main road; turn right to pass the primary school, soon reaching the outskirts of the village.

Corran Sands

Distance 4km **Time** 1 hour 30
Terrain sandy beach, path – boggy in
places, track and minor road
Map OS Explorer 355 **Access** bus from
Feolin to Inverlussa passes the start

**The biggest and possibly the best beach
on Jura can be explored on this very
pleasant circuit, which also follows a
riverside path for inland views of the
island's mountainous Paps – paddling
is obligatory.**

At the north end of the Bay of Small
Isles there is an informal parking area
where a grassy track heads down to the
southern end of Corran Sands, near
Leargybreck – a couple of rubbish bins
mark the turn-off from the road. Whilst
this beach is popular it is rarely busy, even

by Jura standards; the wide arc of fine
sand easily accommodates the handful of
dog walkers, families and one or two
intrepid swimmers that it attracts.

Follow the grassy path at the back of the
bay or walk along the sands. This bay was
once an important deep water anchorage.
Cattle were sent to market via boats
loaded here, the cattle having been
brought from Islay or neighbouring
farms. At the time of the Clearances and
famine, a number of boats took emigrants
to new lives overseas, many ending up in
Australia. If you are walking on the beach,
head up to the path at the back of the bay
once you reach the fence which leads onto
the sands. The path soon goes through a
gate and over a footbridge, crossing the
Corran River.

After a small ford beyond the bridge, pass Corran House and then aim right to the second part of the bay which has a wilder feel with coarser sand. Cross the beach until you meet a small burn flowing out towards the sea. Turn left to follow a track inland, passing the island's landing strip, used for visiting helicopters and emergency medical evacuations. The Paps of Jura can usually be seen clearly from this point. Soon you reach a surfaced road; turn left here and follow the minor road to the three-arch stone bridge over the Corran River. This is the usual starting point for an assault on the Paps and, unless they have formed their own personal cloud, it's a good viewpoint.

Cross the river and take the path to the left on the far side of the bridge to follow the riverside back towards the beach. This path can be boggy in places, especially after heavy rain. If you want to guarantee dry feet it is also possible to continue along the road to return to the start; otherwise follow the path into the woods and then through more open ground dotted with bogcotton. Several benches offer places for a rest, and a boardwalk keeps walkers out of the worst bogs. When the path forks near a bench, keep left to stay close to the river and soon you emerge at Corran Sands, where you bear right to return to the start.

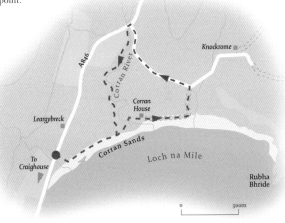

Lowlandman's Bay

Distance 10.5km **Time** 4 hours (round trip)
Terrain farm track, grazing livestock
Map OS Explorer 355 **Access** bus from
Feolin to Inverlussa stops near the start
at Knockrome

This route follows a track across open
grazing land, past a farm and former
lighthouse keepers' houses, to reach a
remote jetty – an ideal site for a spot of
wildlife watching. The track itself has
good views across the bay where seals
can often be seen.

To reach the start take the A846 north
from Craighouse and turn off to the right
towards Ardfernal immediately after the
three-arch bridge. At the small group of
houses at Burnside a signpost indicates
the start of the walk to Lowlandman's
Bay. There is usually parking just a little
further along the road. Start the walk

along the signed track, dog-legging past
the renovated houses to reach open
grazing land. This aims northeast to begin
with, but heads more directly north after a
farm gate. Keep on the main track where a
drive branches off for the Old
Schoolhouse. Lowlandman's Bay and the
Rubha an Leim peninsula which shelters
the bay now come into view. There are
often seals hauled out on the rocks below
at low tide.

In clear weather the Paps of Jura loom
over the island from the left. After a gate,
the track crosses the waters of the
Abhainn a' Gharbh-achaidh which is
lined with hazel and other native trees.
The track climbs gently to reach the
farmhouse at Ardmenish where you
follow it around the far side of the house,
turning sharp right to head away from the
buildings and down towards the sea.

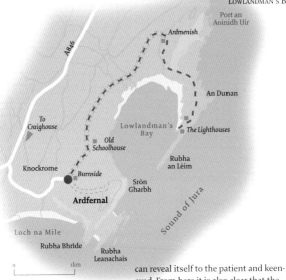

Port an
Aoinidh Uir

Ardmenish

An Dunan

Lowlandman's
Bay

The Lighthouses

To
Craighouse

Old
Schoolhouse

Rubha
an Lèim

Knockrome

Burnside

Sròn
Gharbh

Sound of Jura

Ardfernal

Loch na Mile

Rubha Bhrìde

Rubha
Leanachais

0   1km

The track soon passes through a gate and keeps well back from the water which is fringed with saltmarsh, clumps of grassy turf standing proud from watery channels where the sheep like to graze on the fertile greenery and seaweed. On the left the rocky knoll of An Dunan houses the site of an ancient Iron Age fort.

Keep on the track as it rounds the bay and aims for the Lighthouses. These two houses were once home to the keepers for the lighthouse built out on the skerry at Skervuile to the southeast. Once past the smaller house the track descends to a boathouse and jetty.

This is a wonderful spot to rest and look for wildlife. Apart from passing seals and numerous seabirds, the occasional otter can reveal itself to the patient and keen-eyed. From here it is also clear that the line of rock making up this small peninsula is the same faultline which formed the row of Small Isles that guard the bay at Craighouse.

The best return route is to retrace your steps along the track. It is also possible at low tide to take the more rugged option along the shoreline, although there is no guarantee of dry feet. This return involves grazing land for sheep and cattle and a habitat for groundnesting birds, so is not suitable for dogs. If you do pick your way along the bay, you need to head inland when you meet the outflow of the Abhainn a' Gharbh-achaidh to cross a very rough and pathless area before the remains of a track lead back to the gate and the main track to return to the start.

Coast to Coast

Distance 4km **Time** 1 hour 30
Terrain tracks, minor road, boggy
shoreline, livestock grazing
Map OS Explorer 355 **Access** bus from
Feolin to Inverlussa passes the start

**Crossing Jura at its narrowest point
near Tarbert is a doddle and this
delightful easy walk heads first to Loch
Tarbert in the west and then crosses to
the eastern side of the island to explore
Tarbert Bay.**

The walk starts along the track to Loch
Tarbert from the main A846 road, just
south of the turn-off for Tarbert. If
driving take care not to block any

entrances; there is usually space to park
on the grass verge on the east side of the
road. Begin the walk by following the
track west; the grassland on either side
is popular with groundnesting birds
in summer.

After about 1km into the walk, you
reach the edge of Loch Tarbert. This long
finger of sea loch penetrates far into the
west coast of Jura at this narrow point
and was traditionally used as a haulage
point for boats not wishing to navigate
the Gulf of Corryvreckan at the north end
of the island. At very high tides the track
may become submerged in places here,
but it is usually possible to head as far as

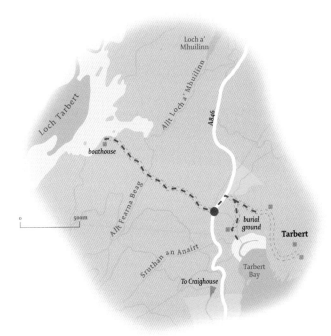

the boathouse which is a good location if you are looking out for otters.

When you have had your fill of this tranquil spot, return along the track to the main road and turn left before taking the turn on the right for Tarbert. Bear right at the junction and follow the track down towards the bay, veering left off the track before you reach the large wooden building. Follow a rough trod through saltmarsh, flag irises and boggy ground to reach the shore of Tarbert Bay, completing the coast to coast crossing of the island.

Return towards the road. From the junction of tracks it is possible to detour across the grassy ground on the right to visit the remains of a chapel dedicated to St Columba and the surrounding burial ground. A prehistoric standing stone, later carved with Christian crosses, also stands here. From the burial ground head up to the Tarbert track, turning left and then left again at the main road to return to the start.

◀ Loch Tarbert boathouse

Glengarrisdale Bay and Maclean's Skull Cave

Distance 10.5km **Time** 4 hours
Terrain rough pathless ground, boggy in places, OS map and good navigation skills needed **Map** OS Explorer 355
Access bus only goes as far as Inverlussa

This tough open country hike crosses from the east to the west of Jura to visit Glengarrisdale Bay where there is an open bothy, small sandy beach, an opportunity to see basking seals and a legendary cave.

Jura is 48km long and grows steadily more remote as the road winds north, passing only a few scattered settlements as it nears the far end. The road is gated at Lealt and becomes much rougher after that, ending after some time at a signed parking area in an old quarry. This is also the starting point for the walk in to Barnhill and for the Gulf of Corryvreckan, so take care to park to maximise space.

Follow the Landrover track north and after 1.5km, approximately 100m short of a metal chain slung across the track, turn off to the left just opposite a small rocky outcrop. There are usually the faint marks of a boggy ATV track which you should follow. These run parallel to the track for a short while before bearing left to aim northwest across open moorland.

Head in this direction for another 1.5km, crossing a small burn and climbing gently to reach a wide, flatter area. The ATV tracks now aim west, eventually reaching a fork; keep to the right side on the more prominent track to climb across the flank of a hill. Loch a' Gheoidh can soon be seen to the south. The route curves northwest, still rising. When the ground levels out, stay on the main ATV track, bearing left where it forks. It soon descends very steeply to pass close to the northern end of Loch Doire na h-Achlaise, a tranquil spot festooned with flowering waterlilies in summer.

Climb the faint track onto a shoulder of a hill and contour across the slope to cross a small col and start the descent into Glengarrisdale. The way ahead

Glengarrisdale
Bay

Sgòrr
Mhòr

‹ Glengarrisdale Bay and bothy

bothy ⌐ cave

Loch
na Conaire

Bàgh Gleann
Speireig

Loch nan
Eilean

Glen Garrisdale

Loch
a' Bhurra

Loch Doire
na h-Achlaise

Loch
a' Gheòidh

Ben
Garrisdale

Glen Lealt

To
Craighouse

0   2km

becomes clearer once down in the glen,
finally curving westwards and descending
onto the remains of the ancient raised
beach. Go through a gap in a drystone
wall (this is easily missed when the
bracken is high in the late summer) and
follow the narrow path to the single tree
and bothy beyond, crossing a burn to
reach the building.

This remote bothy is surprisingly
popular with visitors, those either
undertaking the challenging backpack
along Jura's wild west coast or people
seeking the seclusion of a couple of days
in such a 'get away from it all' location.
The building is maintained by volunteers
from the Mountain Bothy Association and
is open for anyone to stay in. The bothy
book records who has passed by.

Behind the bothy stands a rock which
once formed part of a castle belonging to
the Maclean clan. The chief of the clan
was killed here in 1647 in a battle with the
Campbells of Craignish. Having been dug
up, a human skull and bones were placed
under a rocky overhang just beyond the

bothy and apparently sat there for several
centuries before the skull disappeared in
the 1970s. Opposite the bothy on the far
side of the bay is a cave which is also said
to have held the skull, although this
legend seems less certain. The cave and
bay are certainly worth exploring, and
seals are often spotted in the bay which
has a small area of fine sand near the far
side. The cave has two entrances and is
simply reached via a short clamber
through bracken and boulders. The most
straightforward return route is to carefully
retrace the outward journey, taking care to
try and stay on the ATV tracks which
present much easier going than the
boggy, tussocked surrounding ground.

Barnhill and the Gulf of Corryvreckan

Distance 21km Time 7 hours (round trip)
Terrain track, rough and boggy path,
OS map and navigation skills needed
Map OS Explorer 355 Access bus only goes
as far as Inverlussa

**Trek to the most northerly point on Jura
where a viewpoint overlooks the infamous
site of the Corryvreckan whirlpool. The
route passes Barnhill, where George
Orwell penned his dystopian novel 1984.**

Even if you have limited time on Jura it is
well worth venturing to the far north of
the island. Whilst the less accessible west
coast has rugged cliffs broken by sandy
bays, the east side has a surprising amount
of natural woodland and coastal inlets and
bays beloved of otters. The further you go,
the more distant from civilisation it feels.
Once past the gate at Lealt the road gets
decidedly rougher, shortly ending at a
signed parking area with the distance to
Barnhill and Corryvreckan clearly marked.
Park here and continue on foot along the

track, soon passing a locked chain to deter
any intrepid motorists.

The bleak moorland gives way to sea
views with the mainland visible in good
weather. After around 5km, the white
farmhouse at Barnhill comes into view as
the track starts to descend. It was here in
the late 1940s that George Orwell wrote
his seminal and futuristic book, 1984. At
the time he was suffering from TB and felt
the sea air and isolation would be good
for his health and work. In fact, he and his
young son nearly lost their lives during
this time when their boat was wrecked in
the nearby whirlpool and they had to be
rescued after clinging to a rocky islet.

At the junction with the driveway for
Barnhill, turn left and head north.
Described by Orwell as so remote as to be
'ungetable', Barnhill is available as a
holiday retreat – although a boat, sturdy
legs or a 4X4 would be needed to get there.
As it is a private residence, please respect
the privacy of any occupants and don't be

Scarba

Gulf of Corryvreckan

Carraig Mhòr

Eilean Mòr
Eilean Beag

Glentrosdale Bay

Port an Tiobairt

Aird of Kinuachdrachd

Sgòrr Mhòr

Kinuachdrachd

Beul Leathad

Barnhill
Rubh' an Truisealaich

Loch na Conaire

Loch a' Bhurra

Rubh' a' Bhacain

Loch a' Gheòidh

0   2km

◄ Otter in kelp at Kinuachdrachd

tempted to walk down the drive.

The route now undergoes a distinct change as it leads through a green oasis of woodland – habitat to many small birds. You soon pass the remains of the harbour at Kinuachdrachd, a good spot for a break to look for otters as they fish amongst the kelp. In the early 20th century, five families lived here and a ferry service operated to the mainland until 1932. At the fork for the jetty, keep left and just beyond the bay pass a sign signalling the end of the road. It's not, though, as one more house can be found just beyond the initial steep track. At the top of this section leave the track for a path on the left, signed for Corryvreckan.

This rough trail climbs up through bracken to head between two old gateposts. Seals can often be seen basking on the rocks at Port an Tiobairt far below. The path gets increasingly boggy underfoot – you'll be lucky to get through with dry feet. After the gate with the stile, keep to the left side of a small knoll or, if your energy levels are still high, follow the faint path through the heather which goes up and over it. After descending to a stile and gate in another deer fence the island of Scarba can be seen across the water for the first time.

After the stile the path becomes much less obvious; keep to the right where it forks to contour across the slope ahead.

Bodha a' Chuirn

Glen Lealt

To Craighouse

Climb up the slope and cross a boggy area to the vantage point formed by a couple of rock slabs over the Gulf of Corryvreckan. From here, the swirling waters of this notorious passage are well seen; in the 19th century the Gulf was classed as unnavigable by the Royal Admiralty. The tidal races through the passage combine with an underwater peak and a deep hole and can create remarkable surface effects, including a standing wave and the famous whirlpool – said to be the second largest in the world, though only visible in certain tidal and wind conditions. Return by the same outward route.

Evans' Walk

Distance 17.5km **Time** 7 hours (round trip)
Terrain rough and boggy ground, map
and navigation skills needed
Map OS Explorer 355 **Access** bus from
Feolin to Inverlussa passes the start

Traverse to the west coast of Jura in the
footsteps of the 19th-century laird who
established deer stalking as a sport on the
island. Your destination, Glenbatrick Bay,
is home to a fine sandy beach and an
equally fine summer shooting lodge.

Named after Henry Evans who
revolutionised the management of deer
after taking on the lease of this part of Jura
in 1888, Evans' Walk is one of the very few
routes on Jura marked on the OS map.
Having only one leg, Evans relied on
horses to get him about and so had the
path to Glenbatrick constructed to carry
him and his companions to the west coast.

Start the walk from the fingerpost just
north of Corran Sands and the three-arch
bridge, where there is a small parking area
and information board. Although the
original path of Evans' Walk improves fairly
quickly the first section is mired in
tussocky bog and is best avoided. Take the
more obvious ATV track that leads away
from the signpost heading northwards to
start with. Keep an eye out for a path which
branches off to the left (northwest) part
way up towards Maol nam Fineag. This
soon rejoins the original line of Evans'
Walk and the terrain becomes a little
easier. Looking back towards Craighouse
there are fine views over Small Isles Bay.

Pass through a gap in a line of old iron

Loch Tarbert

Glenbatrick
Bay

Lochan
Mhic-a-phi

Lochan Maol
an t-Sornáich

Glen Batrick

Abhainn Loch na Fudarlaich

Beinn Bhreac

Loch an
Aircill

Loch na
Fudarlaich

Corra Bheinn

Loch na
Cloiche

To
Tarbert

Beinn
an Oir

Beinn
Shiantaidh

Maol nam
Fineag

Beinn
Chaolais

Loch an
t-Sìob'

Paps of Jura

A846

Lowlandman's
Bay

To
Craighouse

Loch na Mile

0   2km

fenceposts and descend slightly to cross over the Allt Braigh an Fheadain on stepping stones. After this the path becomes much easier to follow, as well as drier underfoot. The walk climbs the eastern slopes of Corra Bheinn with views down over Loch na Cloiche and its neighbours. A small cairn marks the highest point of the path which then descends slightly to reach the southern shore of the larger Loch na Fudarlaich.

Walk on past two smaller lochans and stay close to the burn which features several lovely waterfalls and pools, tempting in hot weather if the midges aren't feeling too hungry. Soon the highest of the Paps of Jura, Beinn an Oir, comes into view; this can be a good place to spot golden eagles soaring on the thermals overhead. Keep following the path as it winds its way alongside the burn. When it reaches the Allt Teanga nan Abhainn the route crosses just above the confluence with the Abhainn Loch na Fudarlaich.

The final section heads down Glen Batrick; the path can be overgrown with bracken in high summer. Once the bracken is left behind the path climbs slightly and crosses rougher ground on the west side of the river. The path becomes much more indistinct as it reaches the lip of the raised beach and descends steeply for a short section to cross flat ground and reach the shore just south of the private summer shooting lodge at Glenbatrick. Once you have explored the lovely bay and sandy beach the return route is by the same outward path.

◄ Start of the walk and the Paps of Jura

Beinn an Oir

Distance 13.25km **Time** 6 hours (round trip)
Terrain rough moorland, boggy and
pathless in places, rock and scree,
OS map and navigation skills needed
Map OS **Explorer** 355 **Access** bus from
Feolin to Inverlussa stops at the three-
arch bridge at the start

**The Paps of Jura often take on a mythical
status among hillwalkers, feared for their
ruggedness and admired for their views
and location. This route climbs to the
highest of the peaks and is a must for any
keen fellwalker visiting Jura.**

This route starts from the three-arch
bridge over the Corran River – there is a
parking area just to the north. Begin the
walk by crossing the bridge and
immediately turning right down a path
and over a stile across a deer fence.
The path soon leads to a larger one; turn

left along this. There are many ATV tracks
across the moor ahead, but the line of the
main path is usually clear to follow,
though it is extremely boggy in places.

The path stays high above the river
initially before contouring the slopes to
eventually reach stepping stones near the
outflow of Loch an t-Siob. From here skirt
above the north side of Loch an t-Siob;
there are faint paths for much of the way;
just don't aim to gain too much height at
first. Continue at this angle once you are
past the far end of the loch until it
becomes easier to head directly
northwards, climbing to reach the wide
bealach between Beinn Shiantaidh and
Beinn an Oir.

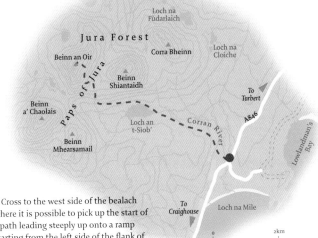

Cross to the west side of the bealach where it is possible to pick up the start of a path leading steeply up onto a ramp starting from the left side of the flank of Beinn an Oir. This path provides a great viewpoint of the most fearsome and steepest-looking pap, Beinn Shiantaidh. From this vantage point it also becomes clear why the Jura Fell Race is regarded as the toughest British hill-running challenge for its approximate 26km distance. The route covers seven peaks and starts and finishes at Craighouse with the men's record currently standing at three hours six minutes and 30 seconds and the women's record only slightly over 30 minutes longer – an epic achievement. Whilst the actual race, which attracts about 200 runners, is held in May, the notoriety and ferociousness of the challenge means the Paps are popular with fellrunners year round and you may well be passed by some on this route.

The path follows the ramp as it curves right and climbs through the heather,

keeping off the scree. Near the vague remains of a stone building the path peters out and it's best to head left here to climb steeply up through a gap in the rocky scree. At the summit ridge the remains of a couple of stone buildings are found. These were used by early pioneers from the Ordnance Survey who used them as their base during the mapping of the Highlands in the 19th century. From here it is only a few strides to the summit where you will hopefully be rewarded by excellent views over the three islands and the other two Paps.

Whilst it is possible to follow a rocky line of descent south from Beinn an Oir, it is a step up in difficulty from the level of routes described in this guide and, therefore, this walk returns by retracing the outward route to the start.

Set out in the Atlantic around 12km north of Islay and a similar distance west of Jura, Colonsay is usually reached via a lengthy ferry journey, frequently disrupted by rough seas in winter. This gives it a remote feel, a real world apart. Its population has grown steadily to around 130 in recent decades as tourism has helped maintain the local economy; several local businesses have been established, including a brewery, a bookshop, publishers and a café.

The island packs a huge variety of natural attractions into a small space, from the justly famed beach at Kiloran to the rugged moors of the interior, from the rocky summit of Carnan Eoin to the perfect sands of Traigh Ban and the rhododendron gardens of Colonsay House. Off the southern coast is Oronsay, site of an ancient priory. Linked to Colonsay by a vast tidal strand, reaching it is a real adventure requiring advance planning with the tide times.

By Traigh Ban ▶

Colonsay

Scalasaig circular

Distance 8km **Time** 4 hours
Terrain minor road, tracks and paths,
pathless ground, boggy in places; can be
overgrown with bracken in high summer
Map OS Explorer 354 **Access** ferry to
Colonsay docks at the start

This varied walk offers a tantalising slice
of the countryside and coastal scenery
that Colonsay has to offer. It starts from
the ferry pier in Scalasaig, which has a
hotel, café, bookstore, brewery and shop;
the route makes an ideal exploration for a
daytrip to the island.

From the ferry pier walk inland and take
the first left to pass the Old Waiting Room
Gallery, following the track up to the
island's café, the Pantry. In front of the
building turn right to go through a metal
gate and take a grassy track until you come
to a telegraph pole with wires going four
ways. Aim left here to climb the steep
ground towards the high monument on
the hilltop ahead. The rough, pathless
ground can be boggy in places and the
final push is easier if you bear right before
doubling back to reach your objective. This
impressive obelisk of red Mull granite was
erected in 1879 to commemorate Duncan
McNeill, 6th Lord Colonsay.

Retrace your steps down to the telegraph
pole and aim northwest towards the
church – easy enough in spring but
impeded by bracken in the summer.

Emerge on a track and follow it to the road, turning left towards the hotel. Here turn right towards the bar entrance but take the left fork (phonebox on your left) to pass the Island Lodges and further houses on the track beyond. Where you meet another track opposite an agricultural shed, turn right to climb uphill on an ancient thoroughfare, passing a standing stone. When you are nearly at the crest of the hill a faint path to the left provides a worthwhile detour, heading first to a mast and then on to the summit of Beinn nan Gudairean for great views over the whole island. Returning to the track, it now drops downhill and soon passes Turraman Loch. At the road bear right to climb a hairpin bend; stay on the tarmac road to the right until the next track on the left which you follow to pass the island's rubbish tip.

A rough path on the left leads around the left side of the fence enclosing the tip; you then aim for a ruined house at Bonaveh. Climb a small bank and continue east to another ruin, crossing rough and boggy ground but following a faint path

along the line of an old stone wall. At Riasg Buidhe a line of ruined cottages is all that remains of a fishing village which was abandoned after the First World War. The remaining inhabitants were moved to modern houses at Glassard near Scalasaig.

Continue towards the coast on pathless ground, then bear right to follow the coast. This area is popular with wild goats – you may spot them, but are more likely to smell them. Keep working your way round the coast, diverting to higher ground to avoid rocky sections and eventually aiming just to the left of the first houses at Glassard. Don't go through the stile here, but keep below the gardens and take a gate in front of a small stone store. This leads to the road; turn left to follow this back into Scalasaig, passing the medical centre and shop on the way.

◀ Ruins of Riasg Buidhe

A ramble to Colonsay House

Distance **8.5km** Time **3 hours (round trip)**
Terrain **minor road, tracks – sometimes
very muddy** Map **OS Explorer 354**
Access **ferry to Colonsay docks at the start**

This traditional route links the main
settlement on the island to Colonsay
House which has a café and fine gardens,
currently open to the public on Weds and
Fri afternoons (check before setting out).
The time given is for returning by the
outward route, but you could follow the
road which is slightly shorter. The walk
can also be extended to take in sandy
Kiloran Bay, near Colonsay House.

Starting from the ferry pier, walk up the
main road heading for the hotel. Scalasaig
is Colonsay's capital and boasts a shop,
village hall, café, hotel, small bookshop
and its own brewery. Turn right at the
hotel as though heading for the bar, but

then bear left onto a track, passing the
phonebox on the left. Go past the lodges
and stay on the rough track past a number
of houses. Opposite an agricultural shed,
turn right to join the route of an ancient
track which climbs away from the houses
and passes a standing stone on your left.
This was once the main route across the
island, but the construction of proper
roads has now made this a peaceful
alternative that is perfect for walkers and
mountain bikers.

Once through a gate there is a faint path
leading off to the left just before the crest
of the hill. This optional detour leads up to
a mast and from there onto the summit of
Beinn nan Gudairean which is a fantastic
viewpoint. At 136m high it qualifies as a
'MacPhie' – one of 20 hills on Colonsay and
Oronsay which are over 91m (300ft) in
height. Many baggers try and complete the

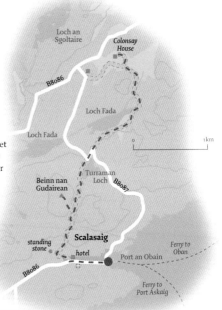

◄ Summit of Beinn nan Gudairean

very tough 32km circuit of all the MacPhies in a single day, the record currently being just under four hours. From this summit return to the track and continue north, soon dropping downhill towards Turraman Loch.

In places the path can be very wet underfoot and small detours may be necessary to keep dry feet. After running alongside the loch, the track reaches the road. Turn right here until the corner of the hairpin bend where you take the continuation of the old track straight ahead. This descends gradually while providing good views over Loch Fada to the left. The wooded grounds of Colonsay House are entered at a cattle grid.

Beyond a gate the path can be boggy but it soon improves, skirting the edge of the woodland. After a sharp left bend, you regain the track; continue ahead, soon passing Avenue Cottage and then ignoring a turn to the left. At the next junction turn right through a pair of old gateposts. Pass the Tobar na Cailliche – marked by an ancient carved stone visible just over the wall on the left and well worth peering over for a glimpse. Just beyond is the entrance to Colonsay House gardens on the left. If you have planned your walk to coincide with the opening times of the gardens and the café, both are excellent.

The gardens have a somewhat overgrown, otherworldly feel to them and are particularly good in the spring when the rhododendrons are in bloom.

To return to Scalasaig, either retrace the outward route or follow the slightly shorter route along the roads if you don't mind pounding the tarmac – traffic is very light. You could also extend the walk by heading to Kiloran Bay on the B8086 - to do this take the path to the right of the tennis court to reach the road and turn right to follow the road to the bay.

Binnein Riabhach

Distance **6km** Time **2 hours 30**
Terrain **rugged coastal walking, pathless
in places, navigation skills needed**
Map **OS Explorer 354** Access **no public
transport to the start**

**Explore the wild and rugged west coast of
Colonsay on this circuit where the cliff
faces teem with seabirds during the
breeding season.**

This walk begins near Lower Kilchattan;
look out for a track which leads along the
north side of the bay at Port Mor. Take the
track and keep straight ahead, passing
onto a smaller track when the main track
turns right. At a gate the route strikes off
over the rocky coastline; bear left and,
after rounding the end of the fence, keep

following the shore westwards, aiming for
the headland of An Rubha.

Just before the headland the fence turns
to the right; follow it here to cross a stile
on the right. After this continue bearing
north to keep parallel with the sea,
crossing a grassy but sometimes muddy
area of ground below a small escarpment.

Soon the route climbs onto the
spectacular clifftop of Druim nam
Faoileann. In the early summer these
cliffs are home to a large population of
breeding seabirds, including razorbills,
kittiwakes and shags – a fantastic place
for birdwatching or photography.

Follow the cliffs as they drop down and
soon it is necessary to take a route further
inland as the way following the coastal

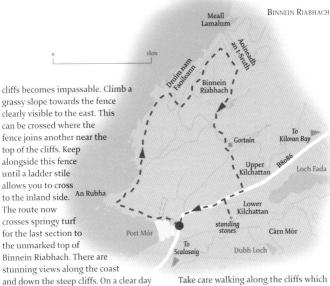

cliffs becomes impassable. Climb a grassy slope towards the fence clearly visible to the east. This can be crossed where the fence joins another near the top of the cliffs. Keep alongside this fence until a ladder stile allows you to cross to the inland side. The route now crosses springy turf for the last section to the unmarked top of Binnein Riabhach. There are stunning views along the coast and down the steep cliffs. On a clear day you may be able to make out the small memorial cairn which tops the next little headland, Meall Lamalum. This commemorates Giuseppe Delgrosso, who perished when the *Arandora Star* was torpedoed and sank in the waters off here in July 1940. The boat was carrying more than 1400 German and Italian internees, as well as some German prisoners of war and 200 allied servicemen bound for Canada. Overloaded and with no markings to distinguish it from a troop carrier it was an obvious target and a human disaster waiting to happen; the lifeboat capacity on board the ship was only 500. Many of those who perished were never recovered, but Delgrosso and a small number of others were washed up on Colonsay and buried on the island.

Take care walking along the cliffs which overhang in places. Continue until forced inland by the deep inlet Aoineadh an t-Sruth. Whilst it is possible from the back of this inlet to carry on through to Uragaig, the going is very tough and it should be undertaken as a day walk with transport arranged. Instead, this route aims south from the inlet, soon reaching a track which quickly becomes clearer underfoot, although it is boggy at times. It bears southwest and passes a small lochan before going through the gate above the cottage at Gortain. Keep to the right of the cottage and follow the driveway down to the road. Turn right here to return to the start. On the way you can detour through a small gate on the left to visit a couple of tall prehistoric standing stones.

◄ Kilchattan Standing Stone

Dun Uragaig and Loch an Sgoltaire

Distance 8.5km **Time** 4 hours
Terrain minor road, pathless coast
and moorland walking, muddy in
places, navigation skills needed
Map OS Explorer 354 **Access** no public
transport to the start

A circuit taking in some of the best of
Colonsay's coast before heading inland
to explore a remote loch. Birdwatching,
beach stops and a picnic could easily
make this into a whole day's outing.

There is a small parking area with picnic
tables near the end of the road at Kiloran
Bay. Continue on foot along the road
towards Uragaig, passing a number of
houses. The population of Colonsay is
currently around 130, though this more
than doubles with visitors during the
holiday season. Keep following the road
as it turns sharp right by Creag nan Ubhal

B&B and becomes a rougher track, passing
a small cottage. Immediately turn
right, signposted for the beach, and
follow the track towards a lone house.
Turn left through a gate onto a grassy
track before you reach the house. On the
far side of the field go through a gate and
bear left to the pebble-filled cove of Port
nam Fliuchan.

The next part of the route climbs up
onto the cliffs to visit the dramatic site of
an Iron Age fort, Dun Uragaig. Once you
have explored the beach return to the
gate, but don't go through it. Walk up
beside the fence and at the top of the
steep section aim to the left to follow a
grassy ATV track west, keeping the fence
on your right. Cross a stile on the right
and a narrow spur of land which links
Dun Uragaig with the rest of the coast. It's
immediately clear why this rocky

◀ View from Dun Uragaig

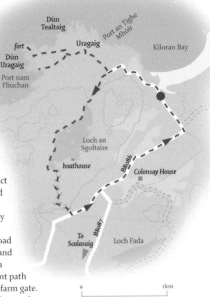

promontory was so strategic, its high vantage point providing sweeping views along the cliffs. The remains of the high wall that sealed the fort from inland invaders can still be seen and behind this the remains of seven buildings have been found. The high cliffs which protect it also provide the perfect habitat for nesting seabirds and it's a great place to birdwatch.

The route now retraces its way back to the road. However, this time instead of following the road round to the left after the B&B and shed, continue ahead through a wooden gate and follow the faint path which bears WSW, aiming for a farm gate. After going through this, take the rough track onto the heather moorland ahead.

Remote Loch nam Sgoltaire is reached after a gate. The path on the west side avoids difficult ground on the east, so bear right to cross the small dam and climb the two stiles to pick up the twisting fishermen's path on the west side of the water. The name of the loch means 'Loch of the Cleaver' and the island in the middle boasts a Victorian summer house on the site of an earlier fort. Near the far end of the loch it is necessary to steer away from the fence to avoid a very wet area – aim for the building, going

through a farm gate and across a burn to reach the building where the route then bends right to follow the access track.

This leads down to the B8086 road; turn left at the cattle grid. Roads on Colonsay are normally very quiet and in late summer the fertile hedgerows will reward you with blackberries and sometimes wild raspberries. Pass the entrance to Colonsay House (the gardens and café are usually open on Wednesday and Friday afternoons and are well worth the short detour) and follow the road back to the start.

Kiloran Bay and Carnan Eoin

Distance 4.25km **Time** 2 hours
Terrain sandy beach, track, pathless
moorland, navigation skills needed,
torch for caves **Map** OS Explorer 354
Access no public transport to the start

Kiloran Bay is often regarded as the best
beach on Colonsay. Popular with families
and surfers, the expanse of golden sand
means there is plenty of room for
everyone, but if you do want to get away
from it all then this climb to the highest
summit on Colonsay, overlooking the
bay, is a great vantage point.

There is a parking area with a picnic
table near the end of the road at Kiloran
Bay. This gives a great view of the sand
and also of the walk's destination, Carnan
Eoin, at the far end of the bay. Start by
heading down through the gate and onto

the sand. It may be necessary to paddle
across the burn which flows out onto the
beach here; if water levels are high this
can be avoided by starting along the track
at the back of the bay which sets off from
the gate near the road corner.

Cross to the far end of the beach, aiming
for a stile in the fence. Before heading
inland alongside the fence, there are some
caves which are worth exploring if the tide
is low enough. These are found after the
next small sandy cove. The one on the
left, known either as Uamh Shiorruidh or
Uamh Heorredh, is quite extensive.

Further in, after the cave splits, the area
on the right has been excavated and was
found to contain a kitchen midden, a
rubbish heap of shells and bones which
provided evidence that humans probably
lived in these caves around 8000 years ago.

◂ Kiloran Bay from Carnan Eoin summit cairn

From the caves, return to the fence and bear left, keeping the fence on your right and soon bearing left at the concrete track that runs across the bay and leads to the farm at Balnahard.

When you reach the telegraph poles, turn right onto a vague path which climbs the grassy ground alongside the poles to reach a shoulder. Here the path to the summit of Carnan Eoin becomes clearer as it bears right and climbs rough ground with ever improving views. The summit itself is topped with a huge cairn with a slightly lower trig point standing a small distance away. At 143m the relatively low height means that this hill does not qualify for many of the hill lists that keen walkers may be working their way through. However, it should be listed as one of the most panoramic summits – the view is truly stunning.

Just to the north you should be able to make out the huge whale sculpture which lies on the raised beach below. The 160m-long outline and initial work was put together by artist Julian Meredith; locals and visitors have been slowly filling in the body of the beast using the stones lying about, while the sheep are keeping the grass at a manageable level. If you are passing, adding a few stones to the tail end of the whale is a great way to while away a few hours and keep children occupied.

The easiest way off the summit is to retrace your steps down to the shoulder and follow the poles back down to the track. Turn left and follow the track as it undulates across the springy turf at the back of the bay to return to the road just a short way south of the parking area. During the summer months this area can be a mass of wildflowers attracting bees, butterflies and other insects.

87

Traigh Ban from Kiloran Bay

Distance 11.5km **Time** 4 hours
Terrain track, pathless section to coast
Map OS Explorer 354 **Access** no public
transport to the start

This gentle walk links Kiloran Bay with the
sheltered and often deserted white sands
of Traigh Ban. It's a delightful spot with
fine coastal scenery and the chance to spy
choughs and corncrakes on the way.

The route starts along the track running
behind Kiloran Bay which leaves the
B8086 just after the sharp corner. If
driving it is usually possible to park just
through the gate; otherwise continue to
the parking area with a picnic table near
the end of the road at Kiloran Bay and
walk back along the road to the track. This
runs over the machair well behind the
yellow sand of Kiloran Bay. At the far end
of the bay the surface changes to concrete

and the track climbs the west side of
Carnan Eoin. After passing through a
rough-hewn cutting in the rock, descend
on the track to the pebbly bay at Port
Sgibinis. Here Colonsay residents and
visitors have been slowly completing a
massive pebble sculpture of a whale using
stones from the raised beach. Although
you can see the outline clearly, the best
view is from the summit of Carnan Eoin
(*see page 86*) just south of here. However,
this route takes in a smaller viewpoint to
get there; bear left from the track to pass
the whale and aim for the prominent
standing stone on the coast at Meall na
Suiridhe. Here, the wild and indented
cliffs are stunning and this is also a good
place to spot passing seabirds.

After returning to the track from the
viewpoint, stay on it to turn a sharp
corner and, before the farmhouse at

◄ Traigh Ban

Balnahard, take the left-hand fork to stay below the house. When the track ends at a large farm shed, the route continues in an ENE direction across the machair and small dunes towards the sea. The fenced enclosure to the left contains the faint ruins of a nunnery, Cille Chatriona, that once stood on this spot.

Once you reach the shore the sandy white beach opens up in both directions. Facing east, the beach is often more sheltered than others on Colonsay and takes in views of the Garvellachs, Seil,

Scarba, the north of Jura, and a glimpse of the Isle of Mull on a clear day.

Although there is no path, it is possible to venture to the northern tip of the island from here, passing another sandy beach on the route. The return walk is by the same outward track; you can detour across Kiloran Bay and then climb up to the road at the far end if you prefer.

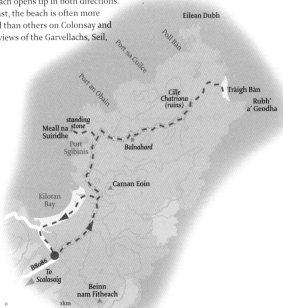

Ardskenish and Dun Ghallain

Distance 9.5km **Time** 3 hours 30
Terrain grassy tracks, paths, boggy in
places **Map** OS Explorer 354
Access no public transport to the start

Explore the southwestern coast of
Colonsay with stretches of flowering
machair, sand, rocky outcrops and an
Iron Age fort on this straightforward
walk from the golf course. Watch out for
low-flying planes as the route skirts the
island's tiny airstrip.

Start from the point where the signed
track for the airstrip leaves the B8086.
There is limited parking on the verge here;
alternatively there may be parking at the
golf course nearby. Walk along the track

until it reaches the fence enclosing the
airfield and then bear right on a grassy
track which skirts the perimeter. The
planes used to land on a grass runway,
but it was upgraded to tarmac in 2006 –
there are currently two flights a week to
and from Oban, taking just under half an
hour. The track curves left and continues
across the golf course – watch out for
players and balls and wait for any shots.
A gate then takes you off the course to
cross open moorland on a track which is
usually quite boggy.

The walk draws nearer to the coast and,
after rounding a crag, the sandy beach of
Plaide Mhor is revealed. Cross to the far
end of the sand and then aim inland

towards the remote farmhouse at Ardskenish. A track skirts round the outbuildings behind the farmhouse and then bends left, leading through a gate into a large field. On a clear day the Paps of Jura can be seen in the distance. At the fork in the track, it makes a nice break to detour to the right and through a gate to explore the lovely sands of Traigh nam Barc. Otherwise continue on the track towards the dunes. The route meanders through the large dune system before

rejoining the outward route at the far end of Plaide Mhor.

On the way back it is possible to climb up Dun Ghallain, the site of an Iron Age fort and a fantastic coastal viewpoint. The fort is located on the small headland, An Aird; you need to cross part of the golf course, a small beach and the boggy ground beyond to reach it and then take the most direct route back to the track, giving way to any golfers. Then follow the outward track back to the main road.

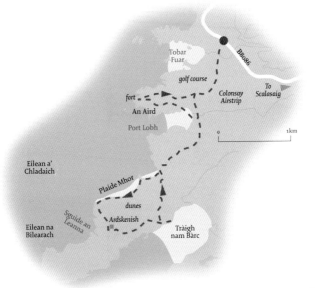

Cable Bay

Distance 7.5km **Time** 3 hours
Terrain minor road, tracks, pathless coast
and moor, navigation skills needed
Map OS Explorer 354 **Access** no public
transport to the start

**Solitude will be your companion on this
remote walk exploring the island's
southern coastline, linking up two sandy
coves and crossing the rough croftland
that still challenges islanders today.**

The Oronsay road (B8085) is reached
just west of Scalasaig and you could easily
walk or cycle to the start point. The route
begins where a track signed for
Baleromindubh House and Cottage leaves
this road. Walk along the track, soon
going through a gate, and remain on the
main route as it drops downhill and
bends to the left to pass the cottage.

Before the house, leave the track and
bear left along the left side of a row of
trees and a stone wall. Head down the
field past a ruined cottage, then aim right
to the far corner of the field; go through a
gate and then left through another gate.
Following the right-hand edge of the
walled field, you eventually reach a gate
on your left. Accompany the large
drystone wall on the right, passing
through this at the gateposts.

The route now follows a lovely section

of coastline, although the
pathless ground can be
boggy and rough underfoot.
Aim east at first and then
southeast to cross a small
burn before picking up a
vague vehicle track which
goes through a gate in a
wall to arrive at a fine
sandy beach. Cross to
the far side of the bay
and then across the
headland of Rubha
Dubh to carry on
along the coast.

In a short while,
the rough, rocky
ground forces you
inland, climbing up
through heather and
bracken, and eventually
aiming for a gap in the fence on
your left. Walk alongside the fence for a
short while before another gap allows you
back on the seaward side; now keep the
fence to your right.

Soon you reach the sandy inlet of Port
na Beiste with its backdrop of dunes.
Follow a path into the dunes on the near
side of the burn to reach the end of a
track. The return route follows this up to
Balerominmhor but, before taking the
track, continue over the dunes to Traigh
an Eacail, also known as Cable Bay. Yet
another of Colonsay's stunning beaches is
revealed, this one with fine views to the

Paps of Jura, although they are often
shrouded in their own mini cloud
system. A perfect spot for a break and
maybe a paddle in the sea, it is also a
good place to watch for otters on a
quiet day.

Return to the grassy track and follow it
back up through a gap in the wall to the
house at Balerominmhor, passing to the
right of the house and eventually
reaching the tarmac where you turn
right to get back to the start.

◄ Beach view near Cable Bay

Oronsay and the Strand

Distance 10km **Time** 4 hours
Terrain tidal crossing, track, coastal
paths; check tide times before
setting out **Map** OS Explorer 354
Access no public transport to the start

A tidal island is always magical, but
Oronsay, accessed by paddling across a
stretch of wet sand at low tide, is doubly
so. Boasting an ancient priory, stunning
beaches, rare birdlife and a feeling of
complete tranquillity, you just need to take
care that you avoid becoming stranded.

A natural causeway of sand and pebbles
links Oronsay to its larger neighbour
Colonsay. Exposed at low tide it is
essential to check the tide times (available
online or at the hotel and post office) and
plan your walk so you are setting out just
as the causeway is unveiled to ensure you
have enough time to explore the island
and get back without being marooned. At
very high tides or during stormy weather
it may not be possible to access Oronsay
at all. You should err on the side of

caution and aim to be back across before
the tide begins to rise as it very quickly
covers the flat sands.

Start from the grassy parking area at the
end of the B8085. Here the Strand
separates the two islands. Once the tide
has receded there are usually pools and
some standing water so barefoot or beach
sandals to protect your feet from sharp
shells and stones are advisable, although
wellies would also work. Tyre tracks can
usually be made out across the sand – the
local postie delivers most days and there
is a small community of around five farm
workers and the occasional residents of
Oronsay House. Aim for a wooden marker
post on the far side of the Strand.

Once across the tidal causeway take the
track which runs along the shoreline and
then heads inland. The farmland here is
managed by the RSPB along wildlife
conservation lines and the habitat
supports both chough and corncrake.

The main track leads you to the remains
of Oronsay Priory, situated just before the

◀ Oronsay

imposing building of Oronsay House. An exploration of the 14th-century Augustinian priory is rewarded with a large collection of well-preserved carved gravestones, cloisters and the Oronsay Cross. This was one of a number carved on Iona and is considered a particularly fine example. It is thought the current priory, which was known to be in existence by 1353 and is dedicated to St Columba, was built on the site of an older religious establishment. Keep an eye out for the gory collection of skull and bones hidden behind perspex in one corner of the ruin.

After the priory go back to the main track and take the first on the right to follow a wide track between stone walls, aiming for the high standing stone ahead. This was erected a few years ago as a memorial to the late I W Colburn, an American architect who, along with his wife, bought the island. Once you've visited the memorial, bear right across the field to a gate giving access to the stunning shoreline.

Head left across the beach to climb the far side next to a small bothy, and follow the seaward side of the wall left to a gate. Go through this and along the grassy track beyond to pass through another gate. After this, bear left on a vague track to head northeast, passing the remains of two

mesolithic shell middens which archaeologists believe may have been markers or had some other social purpose beyond just being rubbish dumps.

At the far corner of the fence, bear northeast towards Seal Cottage which is marked on the map. This remote cottage occupies an enviable remote position overlooking the sand and the nearby dunes are a good place to watch for passing seals and seabirds. Head inland from the cottage on the grassy track and you soon rejoin the outward route. Turn right here to return to the Strand.

Index